# GARDEN CLEMATIS

Stanley B. Whitehead, D.Sc.

# GARDEN
# CLEMATIS

JOHN GIFFORD LIMITED
125 CHARING CROSS ROAD
LONDON, W.C.2

*First published* 1959

REPRINTED 1968

© Stanley B. Whitehead, 1959

PRINTED AND BOUND IN GREAT BRITAIN
BY HOLLEN STREET PRESS LTD
LONDON AND SLOUGH

# CONTENTS

*I*

# THE APPEAL OF THE CLEMATIS

*I know of no family more useful in the garden of
hardy plants than the climbing, shrubby forms of
the clematis . . . of the climbing sorts there can be
had plants of all colours—pure white, deep
blue, pale yellow, purple, and so up to brilliant
scarlet. And they can be had at all seasons.*

CANON ELLACOMBE
*In a Gloucestershire Garden,* 1896

Most gardens with any pretension to distinction boast
one or two Clematis gracing a wall, a pergola, or some form of
support. In all too few gardens, however, are the merits and the
magnificent possibilities of the Clematis fully explored and
worthily developed. Enthusiasm for these delightful flowering
plants too often stops short with the planting of an odd specimen or two, and in their superficial popularity the wonderful
resources of their genus are overlooked.

Nevertheless, the Clematis—using the word for the plural
as well as the singular number, as Clematises is a clumsy
multiplication—comprise one of the few groups of hardy plants
capable of an all-seasons appeal, and of being grown almost
anywhere in temperate gardens. The universality of the
Clematis challenges that of the Rose, and only suffers in that
it is of rather less horticultural antiquity and renown. It may
not offer quite so much reward in fragrance but it has no thorns,
and if the range of flower colours seems limited, new and further
hybridisation promises the exciting and enchanting prospect of
a remedy.

The major appeal of the Clematis lies in the handsome beauty of their flowers and the freedom and abundance with which they are produced. A Clematis in bloom is a queen of the garden to whom all gladly pay tribute. When we add to these floral graces, the readiness of Clematis to flower from an early age, usually at two to three years, to remain in colourful bloom for relatively long periods, and to flower with regularity year by year, it is obvious that the genus is one that can contribute outstandingly to the garden picture.

But their beauty is not solely restricted to the flowers. The foliage is often delicately divided and compound, and in some species, especially the evergreens, of a pleasing texture and colour. Then most species form globose heads of seeds or fruits feathered with silky plumes which persist into the winter, and often make the plants more striking in appearance than when in flower.

To these aesthetic qualities may be added several practical ones. With few exceptions, both species and varieties of Clematis are hardy out of doors in gardens throughout the length of Britain, and are grown widely in America, Australia, Europe, New Zealand and other countries. They can be grown in most soils, for their needs are such that where the native soil is not ideal, it can be readily made suitable. They are particularly worth adopting on chalk which denies so many other beautiful flowering plants to the gardener.

Provided their idiosyncrasies—of which there are few—are catered to, the Clematis are of easy culture, and make no great demand upon a gardener's time and skill, when once established. Moreover, the plants are long-lived, and often capable of rejuvenating and reacting with astonishing vigour to severe cutting-back of older stems.

A final but by no means insignificant virtue, that should be noted, is the relative immunity of Clematis to infectious disease and parasitic pests. Preventive action against slugs and precautionary care against injury to juvenile stems are necessary after planting young specimens, but mal-formed buds, imperfect flowers, discoloured or jaundiced shoots and leaves, are seldom the lot of the Clematis grower, and the plants call for none of the routine fungicidal or insecticidal spraying or dusting which now forms so much a part of modern gardening.

Against the virtues of Clematis, it is surprisingly hard to set any vices or bad points. One may feel some resentment at their drabness and tendency to become untidy in autumn and winter, though this is only true of the deciduous sorts—and only some of these. There is a mysterious disorder known as Clematis Wilt which may cause losses among young plants. And no doubt some gardeners fight shy of the tangle that these climbing plants can become.

It seems probable that the chief reason why we see fewer Clematis in gardens than, say, roses, is the idea that the genus is one of climbing plants and a collection demands a profusion of walls or similar formidable supports. Admittedly, there are few finer ornamental plants for walls, but it is high time the modern gardener gave greater attention to the adaptability of the Clematis to uses in almost all parts of the garden.

There are tall-growing kinds, and smaller ones. Many of them can take their place in shrub borders with great distinction. They can be used to clothe old tree stumps, to grow up through the branches of common trees and shrubs, to form features on their own, to make flower beds, to associate with roses, to grow in pots or tubs, as well as to drape open fences, trellis, pergola and poles. A collection of the finer, perpetual blooming Clematis can become a feature of the garden that never loses charm and distinction.

## THE NAMING OF THE CLEMATIS

A gardener with an etymological turn of mind will find the naming of the Clematis as interesting as the plants themselves. Clematis is the classical and botanical name of the genus, being derived from the Greek κληματις (klēmatis), a name given to several climbing plants and a diminutive of κλῆμα (klema), a vine-branch or twig. It has also been absorbed into the English language as a common name for the plants. This has given rise to a pronunciation problem for the unwary.

In the Greek the letter "e" is long. Consequently the correct pronunciation—if you accept the dictum that "in English words derived from the Greek and Latin the sound of the vowels is decided by the sound in the words of their origin"—is klē′matis, with a long "e". This pronunciation—it is more kleematis than klaymatis—is correct when a plant is being discussed by its botanical name and epithet such as *Clēmatis alpina*. In ordinary conversation, however, when the anglicised name is implied, it is right to say klĕ-matis, with a short "e"; and you have the authority of H. W. Fowler's *Modern English Usage* to back you up in this.

It is when we turn to the nicknames of plants that our etymological fun begins. Among the Clematis, *Clematis vitalba*, the species native to Britain, and to Europe from Germany southward to the Mediterranean and the coast of North Africa, has attracted innumerable sobriquets. Well over two hundred different names have been recorded for it in the different European languages, but there is only room here for the more notable of its English names.

Among the oldest are those of "Ladies' Bower" and "Virgin's Bower". The latter is said to be in honour of Queen Elizabeth I, but others attribute it to the plant bearing the flower of the festival of the Assumption and as such dedicated to the Virgin Mary. Canon Ellacombe, whose opinion on the Clematis heads this chapter, quotes the couplet:

> *When Mary left us here below*
> *The Virgin's Bower begins to blow.*

A botanist and physician to James I, Matthias de L'Obel, named the climber, "Viorna", but by some alchemy of nomenclature this has now become the epithet of *Clematis viorna*, a species native to the eastern states of North America. "Travellers' Joy", a name coined for the native climber by John Gerard, is still popular. It is "Honesty" in many counties, and names such as "Bedwind", "Bedwine", "Bethwind", "Bellywind", and "Blind-Man's-Buff", may sometimes be heard in the West country.

The beautiful silky plumose seed heads that appear in autumn have stimulated native imagination, and the allusions of such names as "Bushy Beard", "Grandfather's Whiskers", "Old Man's Woozard", "Father Time", "Hedge Feathers", "Maiden's Hair", and "Snow-in-Harvest" are obvious. The most common name for the climber in autumn is "Old Man's Beard".

The propensities of the plant to twine around and distort and over-burden the shrubs and trees up which it climbs seem to have inspired such names as "Devil's Guts", "Hag-Rope", and "Devil's Twister", and a country use of its dried-out stems for smoking have earned the names of "Gipsy's Bacca", "Smoking Cane", and "Shepherd's Delight". Other names of so well-known and popular a wilding may be discovered in every county where it grows, but garden usage seems to have settled on "Virgin's Bower", both for *Clematis vitalba*, and many of its specific relations.

# 2

# THE HISTORY OF THE CLEMATIS

> *Clematis—a certain genericke name to all woody*
> *winding plants, having certaine affinitie because*
> *of the spreading branching and semblance of the*
> *vine.*
>
> JOHN GERARD
> *Herball, or Generall Historie of Plants*, 1597

EARLY REFERENCES to the Clematis in man's long association with plants are scanty. The name, as originally given in the Greek, meant a branch or twig of a vine, but later became established as a name for many climbing plants, and as such Pliny mentions several plants as Clematis.

It must be admitted that the Clematis known in the earlier days apparently created no great stir. They find little place in literature. The Bible does not mention them. Neither poets, nor philosophers, nor sculptors, nor artists, have sought to immortalise the Clematis down the ages as they have the Rose. Yet its natural origins are no less profound and rooted in past evolutionary time.

The horticultural history of the Clematis we know today, is most surely charted from about the sixteenth century. The earliest mentions are of the native species, *Clematis vitalba*, referred to as "Hedge-Vine" by William Turner in his *The Names of Herbes* of 1548, and as "Traveller's Joy" by John Gerard in the *Herball* of 1597. No doubt several local names had common and earlier currency.

The first foreign species to be introduced into Britain was probably *Clematis viticella*, sometimes known as the Purple

Virgin's Bower, from Spain in 1569. Since then, we have come to know it in several beautiful forms, and it has played a part in serving as a rootstock for grafted plants of the large flowering hybrids which evolved later.

The English Renaissance in the reign of Elizabeth I bestirred new and lively interest in botany and plants, and witnessed the introduction of a number of Clematis from the continent. In 1573, *C. integrifolia*, a fine herbaceous species with long-stalked, drooping clusters of blue flowers, was brought from Hungary; in 1590, the evergreen climber, *C. cirrhosa*, valued for its winter-flowering, a native of Southern Europe and Asia Minor, and *C. flammula*, with its white fragrant autumn flowers and deciduous habit, also of Southern Europe, came to fill their still honoured places in the Clematis garden; and in 1597, the herbaceous, white flowering *C. recta*, a native of Southern and Eastern Europe, was introduced.

Thereafter there was a hiatus in the flow of new additions until 1726 when *C. crispa*, the somewhat fragile Marsh Clematis of the Southern United States, was introduced, followed by *C. viorna*, the Leather Flower of the Eastern United States, in 1730. A year later, *C. orientalis*, the Yellow Indian Virgin's Bower from the mountains of Northern Asia, arrived.

In the latter half of the eighteenth century several introductions were made: *C. virginiana* of Eastern North America, in 1767; *C. florida* from China in 1776 which lent itself as a parent to many large-flowered garden Clematis later; *C. calycina*, the dainty fern-leaved Clematis, from the Balearic Islands, in 1783; *C. alpina*, the Alpine Virgin's Bower, from the mountains of Central Europe and North East Asia in 1792; and *C. verticillaris*, the somewhat rare Bell Rue of North America, in 1797.

The nineteenth century not only saw the numbers of new Clematis introductions steadily rising, but also the awakenment of the horticultural world to the possibilities of hybridisation.

The opening up of the Far East to increasing commercial and missionary activity was accompanied by a stimulated interest in its vegetation and a flood of plants being introduced to the West; among them several notable Clematis.

China gave the tender evergreen *C. meyeniana*, native to

Hong Kong and the south-eastern provinces, in 1820; the herbaceous *C. heracleifolia* in 1837, and its var. *davidiana* in 1864; the lovely *C. lanuginosa*, one of the important parents of many large-flowered hybrids, in 1850; *C. aethusifolia*, a hardy deciduous climber with yellow bell-shaped flowers, found in North China and Manchuria, in 1855; and the finest of the yellow-flowering species, *C. tangutica*, in 1898.

*C. koreana*, a shrubby plant with yellowish flowers, not much seen nowadays, was collected in Korea in 1820; and collectors brought *C. grata*, a vigorous climber akin to the native *C. vitalba*, in 1831; and *C. montana*, perhaps the best of the white-flowering spring Clematis, in the same year, from the Himalayas.

Japan yielded *C. paniculata*, an autumn-flowering species, in 1860; *C. stans*, a herbaceous type akin to *C. heracleifolia* of China, in the same year; and *C. apiifolia*, another autumn-flowering type, in 1869; but its most valuable contribution was *C. patens*, which became a parent of many fine large-flowered varieties, in 1831.

North-east Asia contributed *C. fusca*, a climber with reddish-brown, woolly flowers, in 1860; and Siberia, *C. songarica*, an herbaceous sort with yellowish-white flowers, in 1880, though neither is much sought after today.

The old world provided *C. campaniflora*, a delightful climber with white bell-shaped flowers, native to Portugal, in 1820; and the new world *C. ligusticifolia*. perhaps best described as a North American 'Traveller's Joy', in 1880; and *C. douglasii*, a herbaceous species of which not much is heard today, in 1889.

A somewhat tender evergreen climber, *C. indivisa*, of some distinction, was introduced from New Zealand in 1840, and grows out of doors in mild localities.

The fever of plant collecting persisted into the twentieth century, and only subsided with the outbreak of the First World War in 1914. This was a period when plant collectors from several countries, such as Prince Henri of France, E. H. Wilson and George Forrest of Britain, ransacked China for its floral treasures. Of the Clematis introduced in the early 1900s, almost all were Chinese natives.

1900 was marked by the introduction of that fine, spring-flowering evergreen climber, *C. armandii*; the less known autumn-flowering deciduous *C. chinensis*; and the late-summer flowering evergreen, *C. quinquefoliolata*. These were followed by the deciduous climber, *C. rehderiana*, with its nodding bells of pale yellow flowers, in 1904; *C. ranunculoides*, a herbaceous species with rose-purple flowers, in 1906; *C. veitchiana*, a climber kindred to *C. rehderiana* with yellowish-white nodding flowers; the evergreen *C. pavoliniana*, a white summer-flowering type resembling *C. armandii*, in 1908; and the deciduous *C. spooneri* with its large white flowers in 1909.

The second decade of our century was marked by the introduction of *C. chrysocoma*, sent home from Yunnan to France by Père Jean M. Delavay in 1884, and thence to England in 1910. In the same year, *C. macropetala*, the delightful lavender-blue flowering deciduous climber, was introduced from North China, and *C. graciliflora*, a June-flowering deciduous climber kindred to *C. montana*.

There is some dispute as to whether the species *C. fargesii*, a deciduous climber with large white flowers on long stalks, now in cultivation in Britain is the true species, or its var. *souliei*, introduced by E. H. Wilson in 1911—to most gardeners a matter of botanical hair-splitting, as the differences are very slight.

*C. napaulensis* (syn. *C. forrestii*), collected on the bordering northern parts of India and China and introduced in 1912, is a vigorous evergreen with clusters of small, silky, creamy-yellow flowers early in the year, that brought this era of exotic Clematis to its end. The 1914–18 war intervened, and only one introduction was added to the species; that of *C. serratifolia*, a deciduous climber, with soft yellow, late summer flowers, somewhat similar to *C. tangutica*, from Korea in 1918.

## THE ADVENT OF CLEMATIS HYBRIDS

While Clematis discoveries were being made abroad, several plantsmen in the countries to which they were introduced set about the fascinating task of creating new and finer flowering forms by breeding, selection and hybridisation. Although several species are now available in improved forms or varieties, it is the hybrids that have made the hardy Clematis of greater interest to gardeners.

One of the first known hybrids was *C.* x *eriostemon*, formerly known as *C.* x *hendersonii*, raised by a Mr. Henderson of the Pine-apple Nursery, St. John's Wood, about 1830, from a crossing of *C. integrifolia* x *C. viticella*. It made long slender shoots each year, dying back in the manner of its first parent each autumn, after producing deep blue flowers in profusion. The cross was evidently also made by others, for the names *C.* x *bergeronii*, *C.* x *chandleri* and *C.* x *intermedia* have been given to it.

In the succeeding years new varieties and hybrids have been raised and introduced by nurserymen in Britain and Europe. A herbaceous hybrid, *C.* x *aromatica*, believed to be the result of a cross between *C. flammula* x *C. integrifolia*, growing stems up to six feet with highly scented, dark bluish-violet flowers, originated about 1845. But the breeding of the admirable, large-flowered varieties so esteemed today centred chiefly around *C. patens*, introduced from Japan in 1836; *C. florida* of China, introduced in 1776; and the South European of 1569, *C. viticella*, when the advent of *C. lanuginosa* from China in 1850 made inter-crossing a rewarding occupation.

Improved varieties of the Japanese *C. patens* are held to have been introduced directly from Japan by a Dutch traveller, Philipp Franz Von Siebold, who was responsible for the sending of the species, and many other Japanese plants, to Europe. Improved seedlings of *C. patens* are recorded as having been raised by various continental nurserymen, such as Victor Lemoine of Nancy and Simon Louis of Metz, but none now seem to be listed.

The honour of producing the first meritorious large-flowered hybrid of *C. lanuginosa* parentage appears to belong to I. Anderson-Henry of Edinburgh, who crossed *C. patens* x *C. lanuginosa* in 1855 to obtain a lavender flowering *C.* x *reginae*, apparently no longer offered. Two other later hybrids from the same Scottish source, the white flowering *C.* x *henryi* and the sky-blue and mauve *C.* x *lawsoniana* are still available today.

The most important advance in Clematis hybrids was made, however, by Messrs. George Jackman and Sons, nurserymen of Woking, Surrey, who used *C. lanuginosa* as a parent with *C.* x *eriostemon* and *C. viticella* in 1858, and from the offspring obtained *C.* x *jackmanii*, with large, rich violet-purple flowers, probably the most famous of all Clematis hybrids; and *C.* x *rubro-violacea*, which has since fallen by the way.

In Britain, the name of Jackman and Clematis have become almost synonymous, for the Woking Nursery has been continuously engaged in raising and introducing new hybrids down to the present day.

Once begun, the breeding of large-flowered Clematis hybrids was taken up by many nurserymen both in Britain and on the continent. Innumerable varieties were raised, named and exhibited, but with the passage of the years, the majority have either gone out of cultivation or have been superseded by better kinds, and you can search the catalogues in vain for many hybrids acclaimed in their day.

The nursery firm, Messrs. Cripps and Sons of Tunbridge Wells, unfortunately no longer in being, raised many fine pale-coloured large flowering varieties, of which "Lady Caroline Neville", a *C. lanuginosa* type, introduced in 1866, and "Star of India" of 1867 have survived, but varieties such as "Marie Lefebvre", "Madame Van Houtte", "Captivation" and "Sensation" are hard to trace.

Another pioneer hybridiser, Charles Noble of Sunningdale, is now chiefly remembered by his "Lady Londesborough" and "Miss Bateman", both of *C. patens* type, introduced in 1869. All that remains listed of the work of the Bagshot firm of G. Baker and Son is "Blue Gem", a *C.* x *lanuginosa* type introduced in 1870.

A similar story can be told of the earlier work done by raisers on the continent. We can search in vain for "Aureliani", a hybrid of *C. lanuginosa* x *C. patens*, hailed for its fine porcelain blue flowers when first released in 1865 by M. Briolay-Goiffon of Orleans. "Gloire de St. Julien" and "Impératrice Eugénie" were introduced in 1867 by a M. Carré of Troyes; "Jeanne d'Arc" by a M. Dauvesse of Orleans in 1869, but would be hard to find today.

Victor Lemoine of Nancy raised several hybrids, of which "Lucie Lemoine", of *C. florida* parentage, was introduced in 1871 and still remains listed. The French firm of Messrs. Bouamy Frères of Lyons gave us *C.* x *durandii* (*C. integrifolia* x *C.* x *jackmanii*), a fine, easily grown deciduous climber, in 1870, and others which are no longer offered by nurserymen.

Since these exciting years of the nineteenth century, hybridisers have been almost continually active in creating finer flowering Clematis for the garden. Their reliance is still largely placed on the blood of *C. lanuginosa* and its initial hybrid, *C.* x *jackmanii* for large-flowering strains. The use of *C. patens* sponsors large-flowering varieties flowering from May onwards, of *C. florida* of varieties which bloom at about the beginning of June. Where *C. viticella* is a parent, large-flowered and small-flowered hybrids have been created, flowering in summer and autumn. The North American *C. texensis* has also been hybridised with the large-flowered types to give rise to highly tinted, beautiful, summer and autumn flowering varieties with bell-shaped flowers.

There is little point in attempting to arrange the innumerable hybrid varieties in chronological order here. Many have been discarded, and such autobiographical details of those now in cultivation are given as far as possible in the lists given in later chapters of this book.

One or two other hybrids and varieties should be noted, however. *C.* x *jouiniana*, a cross between the Chinese herbaceous *C. heracleifolia* and *C. vitalba*, was introduced in 1900, is a delightful vigorous climber, with long panicles of small yellow-white, lilac-tinted flowers in autumn.

*C.* x *rubro-marginata*, the product of *C. flammula* x *C. viticella*, is attractive for its highly fragrant late summer flowers, and fine seed vessels. Another cross involving *C. flammula*, this time with *C. integrifolia*, gave us *C.* x *aromatica*, a very fragrant, herbaceous hybrid, as long ago as 1845.

Two hybrids introduced just before the outbreak of the First

World War that are worth seeking out are *C.* x *jeuneana* (*C. armandii* x *C. pavoliniana*), the offspring of two evergreen species, notable for floriferousness in early spring, and *C.* x *vedrariensis* (*C. chrysocoma* x *C. montana* v. *rubens*), a deciduous, May-flowering climber evolved in France.

# 3

## THE GENUS CLEMATIS

*Clematis—a genus of about 230 species of perennial woody or semi-woody climbers or shrubs, and occasionally perennial herbs, widely distributed in temperate regions but chiefly of the northern hemisphere. Leaves opposite in pairs, without stipules, usually compound, sometimes simple, often with twining petiole or rhachis or ending in tendrils. Flowers solitary or paniculate, actinomorphic, hypogynous, and usually hermaphrodite; with no true petals but valvate sepals, usually 4, but up to 8, more or less petaloid; stamens and carpels numerous. Fruits (achenes) with persistent long plumose or silky haired styles in globose heads.*

BOTANICAL DEFINITION

It is startling at first to find that the genus Clematis contains many more species than the genus Rosa, which consists of about 125 species, and the fact suggests a virtuosity that has yet to be fully explored. Many of the species of Clematis are uncommon and unknown to modern horticulture, others are of doubtful hardiness, and remain unintroduced to us. The hardy Clematis, suitable for the garden or cool greenhouse, with which we are concerned in this book, and which are generally available today, number fewer than 70 species, though there are a respectable legion of varieties and hybrids.

Botanically, the genus Clematis belongs to the Buttercup or Crowfoot family, the *Ranunculaceae*. It is related to such seemingly diverse races as the Hellebores, Delphiniums, Adonis, Meadow Rues, Columbines, Anemones, Paeonies, Monkshood, and Winter Aconites, as well as the Kingcups, Crowfoots, and

Buttercups, among the 48 genera that comprise the full family. They have in common flowers which are perfect, containing both stamens and superior ovary, and of a regular structure, with numerous stamens, usually arranged spirally on a conical receptacle and with anthers shedding their pollen outwards. The flowers are usually nectar-secreting and are normally fertilised by the agency of insects.

Clematis differ, however, from other members of the Ranunculaceae chiefly in that their flowers have no true petals; their leaves are in opposite pairs; and the majority, though not all, of the species make woody climbing plants. Again, although the flowers are normally hermaphrodite, containing both the male stamens and the female ovary, those of a few species, notably in *Clematis indivisa* and *C. virginiana*, are dioecious, having male and female flowers on separate plants.

Botanically, the floral structure and its characters form the most important part of flowering plants by which they are classified. Other characters, however, such as colour and mode of flowering, growth habit, leaf shape and texture, and fruit structure, also furnish significant relationships and differences by which individual species and varieties can be separated and identified.

The genus can, for instance, be broadly divided into (1) non-climbing, herbaceous or sub-shrubby plants; and (2) climbing plants; the latter group being by far the most numerous. Of the first group, less than a handful are in general cultivation, and they are readily recognised by their flowers and leaves (see Key at the end of this chapter).

The second group can be further broken down according to the structure of their flowers into four sections: (a) plants bearing flowers with petaloid staminodes—a ring of petal-like, infertile organs between the sepals and the stamens—which some botanists place in a separate genus, *Atragene*; (b) plants bearing flowers with sepals connivent or with bases wide apart and narrowing or approaching one another towards their apices or tips, so forming an urn-shaped flower—this is also a section sometimes classed as a separate genus, *Viorna*; (c) plants bearing small flowers, seldom more than one inch across, usually white or pinkish, in panicles and rarely solitary; and (d) plants bearing large flowers of 1½ inches or more across.

The further division of these sections can be effected by other easily identified differences in flower, shoot, leaf and growth characters, as is shown in the key given at the end of this chapter. It will be obvious that Clematis plants show much variability in character and habit, making the genus one of the most interesting to cultivate.

Although the flowers of almost all Clematis bear a central tuft of many pistils, surrounded by a ring of numerous stamens, they show astonishing variety in colour, shape, size, form and number of sepals. Some are borne singly, with four sepals, somewhat plain open flowers, as on *Clematis chrysocoma*, others in clusters as in *C. montana*. In *C. florida* and *C. lanuginosa*, the flowers are not only large but have more sepals. In the bell-like flowers of *C. rehderiana*, in their panicles; the solitary, urn-shaped flowers of *C. texensis*, and the rich yellow single flowers of *C. tangutica*, we have a contrast of hanging, nodding blooms, far different from the better known open-faced flowers of most garden Clematis.

Foliage also shows amazing disparity, evergreen in some species, deciduous in most; simple, ovate and small in *C. cirrhosa*, to the compound, pinnate, and long in *C. viticella*. In many of the climbing Clematis, furnished with compound pinnate or ternate leaves, the leaf-stalks and rhachides of the leaflets wrap themselves around convenient supports, acting as tendrils to assist the upward climb of the plant. In colour, Clematis foliage is apt to be somewhat dull and drab when mature, though the fresh glaucous green of *C. tangutica*, and the silky downish yellow-green of *C. spooneri* are attractive, and the dark glossy evergreen leaves of *C. armandii* or the bronzy-purple of the glabrous, fern-like leaves of *C. calycina* catch the eye in winter. The young foliage emerging in spring, whether glabrous or downy with fine hairs, has a delicate charm and tenuousness that one associates with venturing new life.

Several of the Clematis are beautiful in fruit. The fruits consist of small, single-seeded achenes, borne numerously in globose heads, and when the achenes carry long persistent styles, feathered with fine silky hairs, as in such species as *C. alpina, C. tangutica, C. texensis, C. montana,* and the native *C. vitalba,* the plants wear a handsomeness that compares with their appearance when in flower. The seed-heads persist for some time, until well ripened, and loosened by wind and weather, the tailed achenes are dispersed.

It is curious to note that the root system of young Clematis is not unlike one of the plumose seed-heads in form, with many roots spreading out and downward from a common central base.

The natural habit of the climbing Clematis is to clamber up through supporting shrubs and trees to the light, and reaching it, to leaf, flower, and fruit, most profusely in its rays. Consequently, the stems are apt to become bare with a furrowed, fibrous bark, though the young shoots have a soft and almost tender charm, especially when clothed in a feathery down.

It may be said that the natural habit and form of the Clematis have no great beauty, particularly the deciduous kinds in winter. It is, however, part of the art of gardening to improve on Nature, and with good culture, it is possible to make much of the natural grace and qualities with which Clematis are endowed.

# A KEY TO THE
# HARDY GARDEN CLEMATIS

## I. PLANT NON-CLIMBING,
## HERBACEOUS OR SUB-SHRUBBY

A. *Lvs. simple*

1. Lvs. entire, thin; stem 3–4 ft. h.; fls. blue, sometimes violet or white; sep. pointed. *C. integrifolia*

2. Lvs. thick, strongly veined, entire or coarsely toothed; stem woolly, ½–1½ ft. h.; fls. purple; sep. thick, not long pointed, recurving at tip. *C. fremontii*

3. Similar to above; fls. yellow; style very plumose. *C. ochroleuca*

**B.** *Lvs. simple to pinnate*

4. Lvs. or lflts. ovate; stem 6–8 ft. h.; fls. deep blue, stalked, fragrant; sep. spreading.                    *C.* x *eriostemon*

**C.** *Lvs. compound*

SEP. UPRIGHT

5. Lvs. tri-fol., toothed; stem to 3 ft. h.; fls. tubular, blue, in axillary clusters; sep. recurved at tip.          *C. heracleifolia*

6. Similar, but taller; fl. dioecious, deep blue; sep. not recurving.                                           *C. h.* var. *davidiana*

7. Lvs. tri-fol., sharply toothed; fls. tubular, pale blue, in long-stalked, downy clusters; sep. recurving.          *C. stans*

8. Lvs. pinnate; stem ribbed, 1–1½ ft., fl. terminal, solitary, on stout woolly stalk, purple; sep. pointed.          *C. douglasii*

9. Lvs. quin-fol.; lflts. entire; stem 4–6 ft. h.; fls. dark blue-violet, fragrant, in loose, terminal cymes.          *C.* x *aromatica*

SEP. SPREADING

10. Lvs. simple; stem 4–5 ft. h.; fls. yellowish-green, in long-stalked clusters.                                   *C. songarica*

11. Lvs. pinnate; lflts. entire, stalked; fls. white, fragrant, in terminal and axillary panicles.                    *C. recta*

12. Lvs. tri-fol. or pinnate; stem 4–6 ft. h.; fls. solitary or few, purple to pale rose; sep. spreading and recurved.

*C. ranunculoides*

## II. PLANT CLIMBING, WOODY STEMMED

**D.** *Fls. with petaloid staminoides*

13. Lvs. tri-fol., stalked; lflts. glabrous or nearly so, entire to coarsely toothed; fls. purple or purplish-blue, solitary, from nodes of previous year's shoots.                    *C. verticillaris*

14. Lvs. tri-fol.; lflts. toothed, thinly hairy; fls. yellow to reddish-violet, solitary, stalked; sep. ovate-lanceloate. *C. koreana*

15. As 14; flowers yellow.                    *C. koreana* v. *lutea*

16. Lvs. doubly ternate; lflts. coarsely toothed; fls. solitary, blue, violet-blue.                                   *C. macropetala*

17. Lvs. doubly ternate; lflts. coarsely toothed; fls. solitary, stalked, nodding, blue to violet-blue, staminoides spoon-shaped; shoots glabrous.                    *C. alpina*

E. *Fls. with sep. connivent, or more or less upright, and forming a tubular,
urn- or bell-shaped fl.; stamens also upright and appressed, usually hairy*

18. Lvs. pinnate, glaucous; fls. solitary, red, scarlet or carmine,
nodding on stalk; sep. thick, reflexed at tip; styles plumose.

*C. texensis*

19. Lvs. quin- to sept-fol.; glabrous; fls. dull reddish-purple,
solitary on stout, short stalks, pitcher-shaped; sep. thick,
reflexed at tips, pubescent outside. *C. viorna*

20. Lvs. pinnate; lflts. 5–7, entire; fls. solitary, short, stout
stalked, urn-shaped, reddish-brown; sep. reflexed, woolly.

*C. fusca*

21. Lvs. pinnate; lflts. thin, glabrous, 3–7; fls. solitary, bell-
shaped, fragrant, bluish-purple; sep. wavy; achenes without
plumose styles. *C. crispa*

22. Lvs. tri-fol. and pinnate; lflts. lobed, netted and downy
beneath; fls. solitary, urn-shaped, purple-blue; sep. recurved
at tips; achenes with plumose styles. *C. pitcheri*

23. Lvs. tri-fol., or pinnate; lflts. 3–9, finely divided; fls.
solitary on slender stalks, bell-shaped, nodding, pale-yellow.

*C. aethusifolia*

24. Lvs. tri-fol. and pinnate; lflts. coarsely toothed or lobed,
2–5 ins. long; fls. bell-shaped, yellow, fragrant, in panicles;
sep. with tips reflexed. *C. connata*

25. Lvs. ternate or doubly ternate; lflts. 2–4 ins. long; fls. bell-
shaped, dull purple, with silky stamens, in 1 to 3 from leaf axils;
sep. reflexed at tips. *C. lasiandra*

26. Lvs. pinnate; lflts. 7–9, downy, coarsely toothed or lobed;
fls. nodding, bell-shaped, fragrant, pale yellow, in erect downy
panicles; sep. tips recurved. *C. rehderiana*

27. Lvs. doubly pinnate, glabrous; lflts. 20 or more; fls.
nodding, bell-shaped, fragrant, yellowish-white in panicles.

*C. veitchiana*

28. Lvs. pinnate, with many lflts. tri-fol.; fls. widely-bell-
shaped, nodding- white, tinged violet, and stalked; sep.
recurved at tips. *C. campaniflora*

F. *Fls. small, rarely over 1 in. across, white or pinkish, sep. spreading, in
clusters, panicles, cymes or solitary*

29. Lvs. evergreen; lflts. 3 or 5, glabrous; fls. creamy-yellow, silky, in axillary clusters of 8 or 10; stamens purple.

*C. napaulensis*

30. Lvs. tri-fol.; lflts. deeply toothed; fls. dull white, ⅝ in. across, in axillary panicles; sep. downy outside.    *C. apiifolia*

31. Lvs. quin-fol.; lflts. 3 or 5-veined, downy on the mid-rib; fls. white, fragrant, ¾ in. across, in axillary clusters; sep. very narrow.    *C. chinensis*

32. Lvs. variable, tri-fol., doubly pinnate; lflts., small, entire, glabrous; fls. pure white, highly fragrant, ¾–1 in. across, in loose panicles up to 1 ft. long.    *C. flammula*

33. Lvs., quin-fol.; lflts. coarsely toothed; fls. white, 1 in. wide, in terminal and axillary panicles.    *C. grata*

34. Lvs. pinnate; lflts. 5 or 7, coarsely toothed, almost glabrous; fls. white, fragrant, ¾ in. across, in terminal and axillary corymbose panicles.    *C. ligusticifolia*

35. Lvs. tri-fol.; lflts. coarsely and unevenly toothed; fls. dull white, about 1 in. across, in axillary panicles; sep. oblong.

*C. virginiana*

36. Lvs. pinnate; lflts. coarsely toothed to entire, downy; fls. dull white, in terminal and axillary panicles; long, feathery seed styles.    *C. vitalba*

G. *Fls. larger than 1½ in. across, sep. spreading, solitary, in threes, or axillary clusters or panicles*

37. Lvs. pinnate or doubly pinnate; lflts. small, glabrous, glaucous; fls. orange-yellow, solitary or few, slender-stalked; sep. glabrous inside and out.    *C. glauca*

38. As 37, fls. deep orange-yellow, slightly larger at 1¾ ins. across.    *C. glauca* v. *akebioides*

39. Lvs. tri-fol., and pinnate; lflts. ovate, lobed or coarsely toothed, glabrous, somewhat glaucous; fls. yellow, 1½–2 in. across, on slender axillary stalks; sep. pointed, downy.

*C. orientalis*

40. Lvs. pinnate; lflts. toothed or tri-lobed, glaucous; fls. solitary, nodding, rich yellow, of long stalks; sep. to 2 in. long, pointed; seed styles, long, feathery.    *C. tangutica*

41. Similar to 40, with more woolly shoots, smaller leaves, and shorter, blunter sep.     *C. t.* var. *obtusiuscula*

42. Lvs. doubly ternate; lflts. sharply toothed, glabrous; fls. solitary or in twos or threes from leaf axils, soft yellow, 2 in. across.

*C. serratifolia*

43. Lvs. entire, simple, ovate, 3–6 in. long; almost glabrous; fls. dark blue-violet, stamens yellow; 3–4½ in. across.

*C. x durandii*

44. Lvs. doubly ternate, 9 in. long; lflts. downy, sharply toothed; fls. solitary or few on axillary stalks, pure white, 2 to 2½ in. across; sep. usually six.     *C. fargesii*

45. Lvs. tri- or quin-foliate; lflts. entire, 2–4 in. long; fls. solitary on downy stalks, 4–6 in. across; sep. 6–8, pointed; white to pale lilac; seed style, long, leathery.     *C. patens*

46. Lvs. simple or tri-fol., to 5 in. long, woolly beneath; fls. 1 to 3, 4–6 in. across; 6 to 8 sep. oval or obovate, white to lilac.

*C. lanuginosa*

47. Lvs. tri-fol. or simple; fls. usually in threes, 4 to 5 in. across; sep. 4 to 6, rich violet-purple, with bar down middle.

*C. x jackmanii*

48. Lvs. ternate or bi-ternate; lflts., slightly downy beneath, 1 to 2 in. long, entire, or toothed; fls. solitary, 2½ to 3 in. across; sep. 4 to 6, creamy-white, green striped down back, oval.

*C. florida*

49. As 48, but fl. centres of purple staminoides.

*C. f.* var. *sieboldii*

50. Lvs. pinnate; lflts. lanceolate, ¾ to 2½ in. long, often lobed; fls. solitary or several on branched stalks, fragrant, 1½ in. across; sep. 4, blue to rosy-purple.     *C. viticella*

51. Lvs. ternate or pinnate; lflts. toothed, slightly downy; fls. in twos to fours on slender, downy stalks from leaf axils, 1½–2 in. across; sep. white, ovate, 4.     *C. graciliflora*

52. Lvs. tri-fol.; lflts. ovate, toothed, 2–4 in. long, usually glabrous; fls. solitary, stalked, in axillary clusters of 2–5, 2 to 2½ in. across; sep. 4, oval, pure white.     *C. montana*

53. Lvs. tri-fol.; lflts., with shoots, covered with golden down, coarsely toothed; fls. in ones to threes on axillary stalks, 1¾ in. across; sep. 4, white, tinged pink, short-pointed. *C. chrysocoma*

54. Lvs. tri-fol.; lflts. ovate, lobed or coarsely toothed, downy; fls. on slender hairy stalks, 2 to 2½ in. across; sep. 4 to 6, rose.

*C.* x *vedrariensis*

55. Lvs. tri-fol.; lflts. ovate, coarsely toothed, to 3½ in. long, with yellowish down; fls. solitary or in twos, 3 in. across, on long stalks; sep. 4, white, obovate. *C. spooneri*

56. Lvs. tri- or quin-fol.; lflts. ovate, 2–4 in. long, coarsely toothed; fls. in terminal and axillary corymbs, 1½ ins. across, making compound panicles; sep. 4, yellowish-white, fading bluish. *C.* x *jouiniana*

57. Lvs. variable, tri-fol., varying in size and shape; fls. axillary, about 1½ in. across, highly fragrant; 4 to 6 sep. white at base, reddish-violet towards margins. *C.* x *rubro-marginata*

### H. *Lvs. evergreens*

58. Lvs. tri-fol.; lflts. entire, lanceolate, 3 to 5 in. long, 3-veined, dark glossy green, glabrous; fls. axillary in clusters, 2–2½ in. across; sep. 4 to 6, narrowly oblong, white. *C. armandii*

59. Resembling 58; fls. in cymes of 3 to 5 in clusters from leaf axils; sep. 5 or 6, white, pink beneath. *C.* x *jeuneana*

60. Lvs. tri-fol.; lflts. ovate, entire, to 3 in. long; fls. in axillary clusters of 3 to 7, 1½ to 3 in. across; sep. 4, lanceolate, pure white. *C. pavoliniana*

61. Lvs. tri-fol.; lflts. 3-veined, entire, leathery; fls. in large, loose panicles, 1 in. across; sep. 4, white, notched at tip.

*C. meyeniana*

62. Lvs. quin-fol.; lflts. narrow-ovate, 2–4 in. long; fls. in 3-, 5-, and 7-fld. cymes, 1½–2 ins. across; sep. 4 to 6, milky-white, narrow, downy without; seed styles silky, 2–3 in.

*C. quinquefoliolata*

63. Lvs. ternate or doubly ternate, 1½–3 in. long; lflts. coarsely toothed or lobed; fern-like, glabrous, bronzy in winter; fls. solitary, 1½–2 in. across, yellowish-white, spotted red, on short stalk with involucre beneath sep. *C. calycina*

64. Lvs. simple, ovate, coarsely toothed or 3-lobed, 1–2 in. long, glabrous; fls. solitary or in pairs from axils, 1½–2½ in. across; sep. 4, cream, downy without, oval, with involucre beneath. *C. cirrhosa*

matis Nelly Moser. Fast growing to 12 feet. Rosy mauve flowers with bright red . Purple anthers. Flowers in May-June and again September-October.

Clematis Gravetye Beauty. A vigorous climber with cherry red flowers, with cream filaments. Flowers July-October.

Clematis Nelly Moser.

65. Lvs. semi-E, pinnate to doubly ternate; lflts. entire, 3–5-veined, 1½–5 in. long; fls. in terminal and axillary compound panicles, 1½ ft. long to 1 ft. wide; fragrant; sep. 4, white, narrow-oblong.     *C. uncinata*

66. Stems more or less leafless, slender, glabrous, dark green twigs; fls. in axillary clusters of 2–6, on short, downy stalks, about 1 in. wide, fragrant; sep. 4 to 6, green-white.     *C. afoliata*


(ABBREVIATIONS: Lvs. =leaves; lflts. =leaflets;
fls. =flowers; sep. =sepals; -fol. =-foliate)

# 4

## GARDEN HYBRIDS AND VARIETIES

*The Clematis may be looked on as a mine which*
*has not yet become by any means worked out.*

T. MOORE and G. JACKMAN
*The Clematis as a Garden Flower*

GARDENERS REGARD plants somewhat differently from botanists. They are less concerned with precise structural affinities, and more with growth characteristics and culture. When a genus becomes enriched with garden-raised hybrids and varieties, these types of plants are often given a horticultural classification, less scientific perhaps than the botanical, but more practical as a guide to their garden qualities and cultural treatment.

Horticultural classifications of popular genera such as Carnations, Chrysanthemums, Dahlias, Rhododendrons and Roses are well established, and sanctioned by the floral societies devoted to them, and accepted by such authorities as The Royal Horticultural Society. Clematis, unfortunately, have not as yet a society dedicated to their study and culture, and their horticultural grouping is tentative. Nevertheless, the garden hybrids and varieties can be distinguished in ten or eleven groups.

The members of each group are related in that they have a common parentage and similarities in habit of growth and general performance. They may vary in such characteristics as actual flower size, colour, number of sepals, foliage texture or colour, and sometimes in vigour. But they are alike in their basic cultural needs, which is, for the gardener, a valid reason for their horticultural grouping.

The groups are usually named after a dominant parent, and

may be conveniently arranged alphabetically as follows, together with lists of varieties or named hybrids at present in cultivation for reference.

1. ALPINA GROUP. Consists of *Clematis alpina* and its varieties. Deciduous climbers. Flowers—pendulous, bell-shaped, solitary, from previous season's growth in April, May.

   Vars.: *sibirica*; *sibirica* "White Moth"; *sibirica* "Ruby".

2. ARMANDII GROUP. Consists of *C. armandii* and its varieties. Evergreen climbers. Flowers—medium-sized, open-faced, in axillary clusters, from previous season's growth in April, May.

   Vars.: "Apple Blossom"; "Snowdrift".

3. FLORIDA GROUP. Consists of *C. florida*, its varieties and hybrids. Deciduous climbers. Flowers—large, semi-double or double, solitary, on long stalks, from the previous year's growth, in June, July.

   Vars.: *flore pleno*; *sieboldii*.

   | | |
   |---|---|
   | "Barillet Deschamps" | "Enchantress" |
   | "Belle of Woking" | "Lucie Lemoine" |
   | "Charles Lacaux" | "Miss Cavel" |
   | "Comete" | "Mme Alfred Bonneau" |
   | "Coste et Le Brix" | "Proteus" |
   | "Countess of Lovelace" | "Undine" |
   | "Duchess of Edinburgh" | "Ville de Limoges" |

4. JACKMANII GROUP. Consists of the hybrid *C.* x *jackmanii* and its varieties. Deciduous climbers. Flowers—large, open-faced, freely produced, usually in threes, from the current season's growth in July to September.

   Vars.: *alba*; *rubra*; *superba*.

   | | |
   |---|---|
   | "Comtesse de Bouchard" | "Magnifica" |
   | "Gipsy Queen" | "Mrs. Cholmondeley" |
   | "Guiding Star" | "Perle d'Azur" |
   | "Madame Baron-Veillard" | "Star of India" |
   | "Madame Edouard André" | "Victoria" |

5. LANUGINOSA GROUP. Consists of *C. lanuginosa*, its varieties and hybrids. Deciduous climbers. Flowers—large, produced in ones to threes, in succession from short lateral shoots of the current season's growth, June to October.

Vars.: *alba magna*; *henryi*; *candida*.

"Beauty of Richmond"  "Lady Northcliffe"
"Beauty of Worcester"  "La France"
"Belle Nantaise"  "Lord Neville"
"Blue Belle"  "Marie Boisselot"
"Blue Gem"  "Miriam Markham"
"Crimson King"  "Mrs. Bush"
"Duke of Portland"  "Mrs. Hope"
"Elsa Spath"  "Otto Froebel"
"Empress of India"  "Prince Hendrick"
"Fairy Queen"  "Queen Alexandra"
"Gloire de St. Julien"  "Sensation"
"Grand Duchess"  "W. E. Gladstone"
"King Edward VII"  "William Kennett"
"Lady Caroline Neville"

6. MACROPETALA GROUP. Consists of *C. macropetala* and varieties. Deciduous climbers. Flowers—medium to large, solitary, with pointed sepals, from previous year's growth, in May, June.

Vars.: *markhamii* (Markham's Pink).

7. MONTANA GROUP. Consists of *C. montana* and varieties. Deciduous climbers. Flowers—medium-sized, produced singly in axillary clusters from previous year's growth, in May, June.

Vars.: *grandiflora*   *lilacina*
       *rubens*        *wilsonii*
       "Elizabeth"     "Pink Perfection"

8. PATENS GROUP. Consists of *C. patens*, varieties and hybrids. Deciduous climbers. Flowers—large, solitary, from old or ripened growth of previous year, in May, June, July.

Vars.: *grandiflora*.

"Bagatelle"                "Lasurstern"
"Barbara Dibley"           "Marcel Mosser"
"Barbara Jackman"          "Miss Bateman"
"Daniel Deronda"           "Mrs. George Jackman"
"Edouard Desfosse"         "Mrs. P. B. Traux"
"Etoile de Paris"          "Nelly Moser"
"Fair Rosamund"            "The President"
"Lady Londesborough"       "Xerxes"
"La Lorraine"

9. TEXENSIS GROUP. Consists of *C. texensis* and hybrids. Herbaceous, semi-woody climbers. Flowers—bell- or urn-shaped, solitary, produced in masses in succession on shoots of current season's growth in July to September.

Vars.: "Admiration"          "Duchess of York"
       "Countess of Onslow"  "Grace Darling"
       "Duchess of Albany"   "Gravetye Beauty"

10. VITICELLA GROUP. Consists of *C. viticella*, varieties and hybrids. Deciduous climbers. Flowers—solitary or several on branching stalks, from shoots of current year's growth, in July to September.

Vars.: *alba luxurians*    *kermesiana*
       *albiflora*         *nana*
       *coerulea*          *rubra grandiflora*
       *flore-pleno*

The hybrids may be divided into two sub-groups, according to flower size:

Large-flowering:
    Ascotiensis            "Ernest Markham"
    "Huldine"              "Lady Betty Balfour"
    "Ville de Lyon"        "Pourpre Mat"

Small-flowering:
    "Abundance"            "Etoile Violette"
    "Little Nell"          "Minuet"
    "Royal Velours"        "M. Koster"

## 5

# THE GARDEN USES OF CLEMATIS

*These plants have no use in physicke as yet found
out, but are esteemed onely for pleasure, by reason
of the goodly shadow which they make with their
thicke bushing and clyming, as also for the beauty
of the floures, and the pleasant sent or savour of
the same.*

JOHN GERARD
*The Herball*


For the exquisite beauty, graceful form, and varied colour-
ing of their flowers, and for the continuity of their bloom from
the first warm days of spring to the first chilly days of autumn,
the climbing Clematis are, with the possible exception of the
Rose, unrivalled. Yet their versatility goes unremarked, and
possible uses in adorning the garden are neglected.

It is difficult to reason out why so few gardens have anything
like a representative collection of these charming and admirable
plants. Possibly, it is because the culture of Clematis is thought
to present special difficulty, though this is quite untrue. All
plants have their cultural idiosyncrasies which must be
respected if they are to give of their best, but Clematis have
fewer than most flowering plants. Possibly, it is because they
are often considered to be unexciting and untidy in habit when
out of flower, but when well-chosen, well-sited and well-grown,
this criticism becomes invalid.

Under natural conditions, it is the habit of most Clematis to
clamber up and drape themselves over shrubs and small trees.
They grow on the fringes of woodlands, coppices, and glades,

from the feet of their supporting hosts, with their lower parts and roots well-shaded and cool, and their stems reaching into the full sunshine where they flower so freely.

The plants climb by curling their leaf stalks around supporting shoots or twigs within their reach, gripping them firmly.

Consequently, in growing the Clematis in the garden, these two natural needs—a shaded base with a cool root run, and suitable support—should never be forgotten, whether they are placed on walls, pillars, fences, pergolas or posts.

### CLEMATIS ON WALLS

Few climbing plants clothe house and garden walls, porticos and porches, more beautifully and decoratively than the Clematis. Moreover, given adequate support, they are unlikely to place any great strain on the structures. Since every leaf is capable of wrapping its stalk around a support, the plants can anchor themselves at many points, with a stability and firmness that are preventive of damage to their own stems by twisting and cracking.

Support for the plants on walls is most easily arranged by a large-meshed hardwood trellis or of strong galvanized wire. A wood trellis needs to be about six inches square mesh, fitted to the wall with long screws and wooden bobbins that hold it about two to three inches from the wall. If of teak or western red cedar, it will last for many years without requiring repairs, but if less weather-resistant wood is used, this should be treated with a first-class wood preservative that is harmless to the plants.

A wire trellis can be made of horizontal and vertical wires, spaced six inches apart, secured on screw eye-staples, fastened in the wall with Rawlplugs, and standing one and a half inches or two inches from it. Or panels of large, square-mesh galvanized wire fencing, as used in farming, can be secured to the eye-staples.

A trellis, whether of wood or wire, makes it easy to train the Clematis to cover the wall, and to fasten in new growth as it is made. The air space between the trellis and the wall surface is beneficial to growth, since air can circulate through the plants, and growth is not injured by direct contact with rough surfaces.

It is possible, in the sense that it can be done but shouldn't, to fasten the framework of a Clematis on the wall itself, by means of lead-headed nails with a tab, or strips of stout fabric doubled round the stems and nailed to the wall. This brings the stems into direct contact with the wall surface, subjecting them to the risks of damage by abrasion, and close contact with walls which tend to heat up rapidly, and cool just as quickly, is not beneficial to growth. A trellis permits a cushion of air between plant and wall, and what is more telling, makes it possible to display these climbers to perfection.

Although walls are the most popular places for Clematis, they are not always grown on them to their best advantage. Too often the lower part of the plants becomes a tangle of more or less bare stems, ragged and unsightly in autumn and winter, with a top bushiness and over-weightiness of foliage and bloom in the flowering season.

To get the most out of the elegant and colourful display of which these plants are capable, it is essential to train them to fill the space that can be allotted to them, and to abet their natural tendency to climb to the top of their structural support, and then drape it with hanging shoots, laden with flowers. To achieve this effect of a waterfalling sheet of bloom, the trellis support is invaluable.

To cover most walls, it is sufficient to train the stems to fan out over the space available. In using the plants to cover porches or spaces above windows, doorways or along eaves, a single main stem can be trained up to branch and to fill the space where flowering is desired.

Enough space should be allotted to allow each plant freedom to develop its qualities. The amount of space available will determine the choice of plants to a great extent. Although it is possible to control some of the vigorous growers by regular pruning, it is wiser to choose a Clematis that fits its situation in the first place. A workable rule of thumb is to allow each plant a spread equivalent to its height.

Few Clematis climb much above 30 feet. The large-flowered

Hybrids seldom exceed 18 to 20 feet, while many of them grow no more than 10 feet. This does not mean that they need be provided with walls or supports that allow them to attain their limits. They can often be grown on low walls, fences or independent trelliswork, and be trained along the top to cascade down on each side.

Most Clematis are perfectly hardy and will flourish on walls, whatever the aspect. Indeed, a variety such as "Barbara Jackman" is likely to colour more finely on a north or north-west wall than elsewhere.

Some of the early flowering kinds, such as the Armandii group, Macropetala group, Montana group, and species such as *C. chrysocoma*, should have southerly or sheltered aspects in order that the risk of their early flowers being spoilt by spring frosts may be minimised. In gardens which are apt to suffer much from the cold, drying, easterly winds in spring, it is perhaps better to reserve the more exposed walls for summer and autumn flowering kinds. The winter-flowering evergreens, *C. calycina* and *C. cirrhosa*, need a sheltered south wall to develop their blooms freely, while species such as *C. indivisa* and *C. napaulensis* are only hardy enough for sheltered gardens in the south and south-west.

With these reservations, the choice of subjects for growing on walls is very large, since almost all the climbing species, varieties and hybrids are eligible.

The spring-flowering Clematis deserve positions which give them some shelter from the sharp spring frosts which can mar their flowers so much. The danger is greatest when the morning sun catches them clear and bright after a night frost. It is effective in protecting a spring-flowering plant to drape it with string netting or sheet polythene on the nights that frost ·is forecast.

For the highest walls a choice can be made from varieties of the Armandii, Montana and Patens groups, which grow up to 20 to 30 feet. *C. x vedrariensis* and its form "Highdown Variety" and *C. spooneri* are good deciduous May-flowering sorts for up to 20 feet. On low walls, *C. macropetala* and its vars. "Lagoon" and "Markham's Pink", though vigorous growers, should rank as first choices, others are *C. alpina* and its varieties, *C. chryso-coma* and *C. verticillaris*, which reach from six to ten feet.

Summer ushers in most of the invaluable large flowered hybrids of the Florida, Jackmanii, Lanuginosa, Viticella and Texensis groups, with many of them flowering successionally into the autumn, or producing a second flush of bloom in September and October. There is no lack of choice, and the majority have good vigour, up to 10 to 12 feet, and can be accommodated on most walls.

Among the species, flowering periods are often less prolonged, and the plants may climb higher. The Portuguese *C. campani-flora* may reach to 20 feet, bearing its white and violet-tinged bell-shaped flowers in July and August; and *C. veitchiana* of similar vigour, confines its flowering to September and October.

Autumn tends to be a season of few flowers in many gardens, but not among the Clematis. In addition to those giving a repeat of their earlier late spring or summer flowering performance, hybrids of the Viticella groups such as "Huldine", "Lady Betty Balfour", and "Minuet" often give their best display in September and October. *C. flammula* is valuable for its autumn flowers of purest white and great fragrance; *C. orientalis* produces its open, yellow flowers freely to late summer and autumn; while *C. rehderiana* puts out its scented, yellow bells, and the hybrid *C. x jouiniana* blooms profusely with small, white to yellow, star-like flowers in panicles.

It is also possible to have a sequence of bloom through the winter on the well-sheltered walls of mild gardens. *C. calycina*, the evergreen climber of 12 to 15 feet, will produce its creamy-white, nodding flowers, freckled with reddish spots inside, from November to February, and its fernlike, finely divided, bronzy-purple foliage is attractive. *C. cirrhosa*, another evergreen, produces creamy-yellow, hanging flowers in pairs from January to March and the hybrid, *C. x jeuneana* bridges winter and spring with its many-flowered cymes of white, pink-tinted, dainty blooms. In the warmest of the counties, *C. napaulensis* can be grown in a well-sheltered corner for its winter clusters of small, creamy-yellow flowers, with purple stamens.

# The Garden Uses of Clematis

## CLEMATIS FOR PILLARS, POSTS AND PERGOLAS

Few gardens have sufficient wall space to take more than a few Clematis, but a collection can be greatly increased by growing the plants on pillars, posts and pergolas.

The large-flowered hybrids, which flower freely and continuously over a period, make colourful columns of great and striking beauty when grown to drape pillars, which may consist of thick-sectioned posts, or better still, of tripods or quadrapods made of stout hardwood poles, treated with a wood preservative for long life, or of a rot-resistant timber such as western red cedar. These pillars can be placed as features along walks, at the backs of borders, or to grace lawns and courtyards. An alternative method is to space three to four poles equidistances apart, and grow the plant with its shoots trained around and about them, with a more or less open centre.

Hybrids of the Jackmanii and Lanuginosa groups lend themselves admirably to pillar-growing, though others may also be tried. The object, however, is to clothe the supports with bloom from base to crown, and to do this effectively the plants must be properly trained and tended. Newly planted specimens must be severely cut back to within four or six inches of their base in order to induce several stems to start low down. It is helpful to train these stems to twine or wrap themselves with a slowly ascending spiral around their supports, as the bending encourages the laterals to break into flowering stems.

It is necessary to give some purchase to the plants to which the twisting leaf stalks can attach themselves. A good plan is to give a smooth pillar an outer sleeve of wire-netting, while poles can be left with side branches pruned to stubs instead of flush. If sawn wood is used, it is worth while studding the supports with hardwood dowels projecting from the wood, to which the plants can cling.

As the plants climb to the top of their supports, the lateral growths will lengthen and drape down on all sides with cascades of bloom. To maintain the plant in good vigour and continuous bloom for their flowering period, they must have proper attention at the right times in such matters as pruning and manuring, which are discussed in later chapters.

Many varieties of the Clematis can be trained up tall poles or posts, with their blooming shoots hanging from the upper limits. With the more vigorous sorts, however, this is apt to produce a top-heavy feature, none too stable in wind, and none too graceful in appearance. If care is taken to choose a post that can accommodate the specimen plant to the limit of its mature height, the effect can be pleasing. An alternative is to fit the head of the post with an umbrella-like framework on which the stems can spread. This framework can droop like the ortho-dox opened umbrella or flare upwards like an umbrella blown inside out. Secure anchorage for the post can be assured by cross-pieces at the foot buried in the ground, or by setting the post in concrete.

Smaller flowering Clematis, such as those of the Montana group, can be used to grace posts linked across the tops by steel chain, wood cross-pieces, or strong, stranded galvanised wire. They thread themselves along the links and soon make thick ropes of their growth, covered with flowers at blossoming time.

A pergola gives an ideal support for all kinds of climbing Clematis, since freedom to ramble over the top of the structure encourages their natural proclivity. Moreover, the plants dress the pergola with great charm and effectiveness when in flower.

### CLEMATIS WITH SHRUBS AND TREES

In nature, Clematis grow in association with shrubs and trees, growing into and through them by means of their clasping leaf petioles, and this way of growing them is worth exploiting in the garden. Since the plants have adjusted themselves naturally to compete and hold their own with tree roots in the soil, there is little difficulty in establishing them. Although they cling tenaciously to twigs and branches, their stems do not twine tightly and hug their host to death in the same way as Honey-suckle often does.

The chief danger is that in time the top hamper of the climber may become too weighty to be borne in a period of high wind or rumbustious weather. To avoid this, the Clematis should be matched to the supporting host. The strong-growing *C. montana* and its varieties, for instance, require a stouter and taller growing tree than the slighter *C. flammula*.

Naturally, all the climbing Clematis are ready to clamber into shrubs and trees, forming in time their own twisted rope-like strands of stems, and clothing their hosts with their drapery of hanging shoots which turn them into bowers of delightful colour when in flower.

The smaller trees, such as Thorns, Laburnums and Rowans, make good hosts for Clematis, and if they fork near the ground so much the better. The more vigorous sorts, such as *C. montana*, require a fairly tall-growing host, and are very pleasing in company with Holly. Large deciduous and evergreen shrubs, which may not in themselves be of great ornamental value, can be used as hosts to Clematis. The large-flowered hybrids may be grown in vivid display in this way. Care should be taken, how-ever, against clothing a shrub with brittle wood with too prolific a Clematis.

One of the most delightful Clematis to grow with a tall, strong shrub is *C. rehderiana*; its long shoots being dressed in panicles of fragrant, pale yellow, nodding flower beds in the autumn. Other species of great charm for draping shrubs and trees are the highly scented *C. flammula*, with its purest white, small flowers freely borne in loose panicles; *C. viticella* and its several forms; and the graceful *C. campaniflora*, its flowers nod-ding with petals recurved, dainty and fragile, but in great profusion.

*C. paniculata*, with its hawthorn-scented panicles of small white flowers, is one of the last of the Clematis to flower in autumn, and will do so all the better protected by a large shrub or Holly in a sheltered part of the garden.

Some of the Clematis are as attractive for their silky plumes of seed-heads as for their flowers, and *C. tangutica* (Graverye var.), *C. spooneri*, and *C. macropetala* are all beautiful in this respect when climbing through their plant hosts.

Climbers of lesser vigour, suitable for clothing unimportant shrubs of six to ten feet, may be chosen from *C. alpina* and its vars., *C. crispa*, *C.* x *durandii* and hybrids of the Lanuginosa, Texensis and Patens groups.

Another place where Clematis may be planted to grow naturally is at the foot of hedges that are left more or less un-pruned. Here, climbers like *C. montana* will run along the top with shoots waterfalling to either side, and breaking into a tablecloth of colour each spring. On hedges subject to regular pruning, it is less practical to grow Clematis in them, as mutilation, when flowering is taking place or imminent, is difficult to avoid.

### CLEMATIS WITH OTHER CLIMBERS

Just as they will climb readily into shrubs and trees, so will Clematis climb through and among other climbers on walls, pillars and similar supports. They can be grown in association with ornamental vines (*Vitis, Parthenocissus*, etc.) in perfect amity. They may also be grown in company with climbing pillar roses, and the climbing hybrid tea roses; and the combination of a large-flowering Clematis such as "Belle of Woking" with a climbing "Gloire de Dijon" is a suggestion for a superb picture in early summer. It is, however, unwise from a practical point of view to grow them with the Rambler Roses, since the pruning of the latter entails cutting away the flowered shoots to ground level or nearly so, and presents difficulty in removing them.

### CLEMATIS FOR COVER

The profuse production of shoots and flowers each season makes the climbing Clematis ideal cover for objects that may otherwise be eye-sores in the garden. They can, for instance, be used to mask sheds or outbuildings, trained to run up to and over the roof. They make admirable cover for old tree stumps and may be planted in the wild garden to turn dull coverts or nondescript bushes into mounds and hummocks of colour.

Before planting Clematis at the foot of tree stumps, it is useful to paint the wood thoroughly with a wood preservative

(Cuprinol, Presotim, etc., but not creosote) to prevent its premature rotting by fungi, and to provide a sleeve of wire netting or a few rings of pegs to which the plants can cling. The roots of the Clematis should be planted on the shady side of the stump, and the stems pruned to break into several shoots low down which can be trained up the stump on all sides.

On tall stumps or dead trees which have been left standing, vigorous types of Clematis such as *C. montana*, *C. grata*, *C. paniculata*, *C. rehderiana* and *C.* x *vedrariensis* offer a choice that will grow to 30 feet or more. On shorter stumps, almost any of the large-flowered hybrids will create a delightful picture.

It is becoming rare for new gardens to be made out of land on which forest trees have been felled, leaving roots and bases to be dug out. Such roots, tilted on their sides, were commonly used to form what Victorians called a "rootery". Where they are available today, they can be conveniently arranged in line, arc, square or circle, and made into picturesque features with Clematis planted to clamber over them.

In gardens containing immovable boulders or rocks, Clematis can again be used successfully to clothe the bare rock faces, the stems being trained to the top and then allowed to sprawl and hang over with pendant shoots. This is a much more pleasing way of covering rock than using Ivy.

### CLEMATIS IN BEDS AND BORDERS

The facility with which Clematis will grow horizontally over the ground as well as vertically up walls and supports has long been known and too little exploited. Nevertheless, Clematis, used as bedding plants, make striking and colourful ornamental jewels for any garden setting. They have the advantages of being permanent, flourishing with greater vigour and beauty each succeeding year, and yet entailing less care and attention than the average Rose bed. Moreover, with proper attention, their flowering period is long, and the spectacle of a bed of large-flowering Clematis producing its velvety-soft blooms in their varied hues with profusion is a sight to look forward to with increasing excitement year after year.

Clematis beds can be made compelling features set in lawns, giving a glow to any corner, or as a long bed to one or more sides. They are splendid centre carpets for forecourts, and can be arranged around statues, fountains, or sun-dials with a grace and glow that out-rivals the more conventional Rose or annual bedding stock. They are adaptable to the more geometrical beds of the formal stone-paved garden.

The needs of bedded-out Clematis are few though essential. The first is a well-lighted position, open to the sun for most of the day. The second is a thoroughly prepared soil, which must be well-drained, well provided with organic matter, and a modicum of lime or chalk. An annual replenishment of plant food, a judicious help to foster growth in unfavourable weather such as watering in drought, and ordered, regular pruning are their general cultural needs.

There are broadly two ways of bedding Clematis; they can be grown to spread over the surface of the ground itself, or over a low framework raising them out of direct contact with the soil. In the first method, the initial branches of the plant should be spread and arranged so that the young shoots will cover the bed, and they in their turn are pegged down as they grow and before they become inter-tangled with one another. At flowering time, blooms are borne all along their length, transforming the bed into a brilliant cushion of flowers. The effect is vivid and rewarding, whether the bed is flat or rounded.

The second method gives a raised effect, that is gorgeous at a distance as well as near-to. It can be achieved by firmly inserting bare branches of a rot-resistant wood such as Yew, Scots Fir or Cedar at an angle in the soil to provide a domed framework through and on which the Clematis shoots can scramble; or a frame of rot-proofed timber or rods can be provided. A heap of pea-sticks may even be used for a season or so, though they are not very permanent. A Clematis bed can also be raised by mounding rubble or rubbish such as stones or large-sized clinker in the centre, and training plants to rove over this.

The plants should be chosen according to the size of the bed.

*Clematis armandii*

*Clematis montana*

Small beds, of six to ten feet across, can be filled with a single plant if the shoots are pegged out to fill the space available. Flowers are not produced near the base of plants, however, and it is generally more effective to plant more than one Clematis so that flowering shoots of one plant may grow and cover the base of another, making the whole bed a sea of colour.

In large beds, the permanent plants should be spaced six to eight feet apart, in the case of most varieties; strong growers can be placed 10 to 12 feet. At the outset, however, in order to give a full flowering effect for the first two or three years, double the number of young plants can be set, and the superfluous removed later.

In planting, care should be taken to set the plants chosen for bedding at an angle, so that there is a minimum risk of the young stems becoming kinked or easily broken.

A Clematis bed will have a tendency to look somewhat bare, especially at the edges, in winter. This can be avoided by planting edges of suitable dwarf shrubs. Lavender, dwarf Box, dwarf Euonymus, Santolina, and *Erica carnea* in its varieties, are suggestions that come readily to mind. The last are especially useful as they give colour in winter. The barren look of a Clematis bed in late winter is no worse than that of a Rose bed, and can be cheerfully relieved by the planting of early flowering bulbs such as Snowdrops, Crocuses, Winter Aconites, Grape Hyacinths, Chionodoxas, Snowflakes, and similar subjects which can be left undisturbed to multiply for several years.

The most effective Clematis for beds belong to the summer and autumn flowering kinds, particularly those of the Jackmanii group such as *C. x jackmanii* itself, and its varieties, *praecox*, *rubra* and *superba*, "Comtesse de Bouchaud", "Perle d'Azur", "Star of India" and "Victoria"; and of the Lanuginosa group such as "Beauty of Worcester", "Blue Belle", "Blue Gem", "Crimson King", "Fairy Queen", "Henryi", "Lady Northcliffe", "Marie Boisselot", "Mrs. Hope", "Prince Hendrick", "W. R. Gladstone", and "William Kennet".

These types produce their flowers most freely from shoots of the current year's growth. After planting, they should be cut back to within 24 inches of their base about February, and the subsequent shoots trained to give a framework of branches; in turn these are pruned back to five to seven feet from the base in the second February. By then, a framework of branches will be in being. Subsequent treatment calls for some training of the shoots as they are made, and then an annual cutting back of these shoots to within five or six inches of their base, immediately above a node.

It is permissible, after the first flush of flowers, to prune the flowered shoots back by one half or one third, with a view to stimulating new flowering growth for another display. If this is done, some invigoration of the plants by liquid feeding is helpful to maintain vigour.

For earlier flowering in spring, some of the Patens group of Clematis can be used, such as "Barbara Dibley", "Barbara Jackman", "Edouard Desfosse", "Fair Rosamund", "Lady Londesborough", "Lasurstern", "Miss Bateman", "Nelly Moser", "Mrs. P. B. Truax" and "The President". These kinds flower from the old wood; giving a most pleasing display in May and June. After flowering, the flowers should be cut off at the first good buds beneath them, and the wood then left to ripen in the light and air. Greater trouble needs to be taken in training the branches of these spring-flowering Clematis when used for bedding, or they get into a sad tangle. They have little to offer during the summer, however, though some may flower again in September. The beds can be made gay and colourful for the summer by planting out flowering plants in pots, such as Fuchsias or Pelargoniums, among them.

A new dimension can be given to any flat or domed bed of Clematis by permitting one plant to grow upright, with shoots climbing a simple tripod of wooden supports or similar structure. It could be a different type to the plants forming the bed, or be formed from some of the shoots of one of the bedding plants. Such an accent needs careful placing, however, and would be more distinctive if, offset to the side and/or the back of the bed rather than in the centre or in symmetry with the proportions of the bed. The support itself need not be so very tall, under the circumstances.

## The Garden Uses of Clematis

There is no reason why the types of Clematis suitable for bedding should not also be planted in the flower border, growing on suitable firm supports. Their abundance of bloom over a lengthy period makes them valuable subjects for the back third of any border broad enough to contain them. They associate well with tall-growing herbaceous plants such as Delphiniums, Hollyhocks and Monkshood, and a selection of both spring and summer flowering sorts assure border background colour for the greater part of the growing season. The trenching, organic manuring and soil preparation that suits herbaceous perennials meets the needs of the Clematis, with the addition of lime, chalk or mortar rubble to the soil about their roots, and the climbers thrive on the same attention as that given to Clematis in beds.

Banks are often difficult places to cultivate satisfactorily in gardens. They can be made gay and pleasing, however, by planting Clematis at their feet, with shoots trained and pegged in place to cover their faces. It is also possible to use Clematis as an edging plant, growing horizontally, with its shoots confined to a line, and making a low hedge of floral colour in due season. Such an edging is much more pleasing than the Ivy sometimes used.

### Planning a Clematis Garden

So varied and adaptable a race of flowering plants as the Clematis is worthy of greater appreciation by garden lovers than it commonly receives. At present it seems to be deemed sufficient to grow a few members here and there in a garden, and except in a few discerning exceptions, gardeners have yet to awaken to the possibilities of Clematis in furnishing space devoted to them alone. After all, we are accustomed to giving other flowers such as Roses, Rhododendrons, Azaleas, Heaths, and Alpines, gardens on their own. Why do we continue to overlook the breath-taking glory possible by planning and planting a Clematis garden?

The genus is one full of delightful species and innumerable and exceptionally beautiful varieties and hybrids with the promise of a season of bloom that is longer than that of any other comparable flowering race of perennial plants. A garden given to a collection of Clematis is still sufficiently out of the ordinary as to be almost unique. It provides floral colour for the so-called dog days of June when spring-flowering shrubs are spent, and there is a check in the tide of seasonal bloom. Once planted, it entails no great cost in upkeep, and is demanding of no inexorable routines or emergency treatments in pest or disease control. While a Clematis garden can be established on almost any soil, it is the ideal feature or speciality for those who garden on limestone or chalk.

Some of the ways in which Clematis can be grown have already been indicated in this chapter. The planning of a Clematis garden calls for a combination of the growing methods suited to the space available. Although the plants should have adequate room in which to display their qualities, the differences in vigour and height are such that there is ample choice for limited space and the unlimited.

In the average small garden, a Clematis feature can often be made in one or more corners. The corner may be framed with upright posts linked by top rails and braced across the angles with more rails, and on this framework a selection of the taller climbers can be grown. Within the angle of the corner, a Clematis bed can be made, for plants to grow horizontally, and in which provision can also be made for one or more of the shorter kinds, such as *C. macropetala* or *C. alpina*, to be grown on short wood tripods. Such a feature would make a more colourful background and framing of a small garden than the more customary one of small flowering trees and shrubs.

With more space available, the Clematis planting can be extended into a full garden border. Here, in addition to the tall trellis or wood frame of supports for the more vigorous plants, full use can be made of species and varieties of differing stature in the border itself. Some may be trained up tripods or stout rods arranged in squares, triangles or circles to their full height, others given less tall support, so that their flowering shoots may hang and drape with a contrasting effect. The floor of the border can be covered with horizontally trained plants.

Further variety may be introduced by the use of the herbaceous Clematis with their handsome foliage and untypical flowers.

Other places where it is possible to grow a small collection of Clematis together are at the base of walls or fences, where a border at the foot can be extended, and around the central feature of a pergola, rotunda or bower.

The most representative collections, however, need a fair amount of room, and where this can be afforded, a Clematis garden can be laid out after the general pattern of a Rose garden, though with greater provision for the climbing character of the plants. There is a similar need for beds, though for Clematis they should not be less than eight to ten feet wide. The design may be formal or informal, with pathways of stone, brick, gravel or grass to divide and give access to the beds.

The garden can be enclosed by a frame of rustic or trellis on which species and choice varieties can be grown. At intervals, this frame may be interrupted by wide, graceful arches over which the more vigorous large-flowering hybrids may be trained. A central feature can also be made of tall-growing Clematis, though the shape this should take is a matter for individual imaginative treatment. It can take the form of a fairly large circle of posts and cross-pieces, up which a selection of Clematis can be grown in colour harmony; or the form of a cross of stout square-meshed trellis, which, if double-walled, allows at least two different types to be grown back-to-back on each wing.

Alcoves, backed by wood-framework or trellis, provide further sites, and pergolas and arches can be tastefully used over the walks. These various means of support need not cater for the full potential height of the plants, for when they do not, the plants will drape their shoots down with telling effect. Single or tripod supports can be used in or at the corners of beds, surmounted with umbrella-shaped or spreading frames to provide for the mushroom-like habit of growth, with the shoots spreading over the tops and then falling gracefully on all sides.

The beds themselves are best reserved for the large-flowered hybrids, planted and grown on the lines already described. There is tremendous scope in such developments for individual innovation and experiment. A Clematis garden cannot fail to possess a natural beauty that evolves from the graceful habit of the plants, and throughout the season there is always a picture of enchanting bloom and softening foliage, masking the soil on the ground, and stimulating the play of light and shade at varying heights up to the skyline.

In a Clematis garden it is possible to plant for enjoyment and interest throughout the year; the summer-flowering large-flowered hybrids following the smaller-flowered spring-blooming *C. alpina, C. montana, C. macropetala* and *C. patens* types, and in turn being followed by the autumn-flowering *C. texensis* and *C. viticella* kinds; and the charming loveliness of those species which carry silky seed heads. For winter, there are the evergreens with their shining foliage, and early flowers.

There are many colour combinations which can be indulged to suit personal tastes. The white-flowering varieties go perfectly with any of the coloured. Care is needed, however, to see that the richer, deeper purples are not allowed to dull and over-rule the more delicate lavender-blues, especially when the latter are used in beds. Again, when the small-flowered type is grown in association with large-flowered hybrids, it is best to grow it in a manner that gives it a separate distinction, as would be conferred by letting it climb above the level of a bed of the large-flowered kind.

A possible criticism of a garden devoted entirely to Clematis can be aimed at its appearance in winter. It is true that the bare and tangled-looking warp of the stems of the deciduous kinds have a dead, ragged and somewhat dreary look in the time of their dormancy. But, as mentioned earlier, a Clematis garden in winter is no more depressing than one devoted to Roses, while the beauty with which it comes to life at the first breath of spring is one of the most refreshing miracles of plant life.

This look of winter bareness can, however, be relieved by a judicious planting of the evergreen types, and by a liberal planting of early flowering bulbs as already suggested for

Clematis beds. It is equally possible to plant some of the dwarf-growing shrubs and herbaceous border flowers of short to medium height, when accents of contrasting colour, or additional cover, is required.

# 6

## SOILS AND THEIR PREPARATION

*The Earth, gentle and indulgent, ever subservient
to the wants of man, spreads his walks with
flowers.*

PLINY II
*The Natural History, I. ii.* A.D. 23–79

To MAKE the numerous long shoots, well furnished with
leaves, and to produce flowers abundantly, season after season,
the Clematis plant must have the assistance of a highly active
and exceptionally strong root system. In fact, the climbing
Clematis is equipped naturally with roots of a fleshy character,
radiating in number from the base of the stem, capable of
rapid elongated growth that can penetrate widely and deeply
and hold their own with the roots of competing plants nearby,
in congenial soil.

In Nature, plants adapt themselves to their habitats or perish.
Clematis, like thousands of other genera and species, had
been doing this for thousands of years before Man took to
gardening. Some consideration, therefore, of the conditions
under which plants grow naturally furnishes clues as to their
natural likes and dislikes which we can only ignore at our peril.

When found wild, Clematis usually grow near the bases of
shrubs and trees where the soil in which they root is well-drained
and aerated, yet moist both by reason of the shade cast by the
taller plants, and of the layer of organic matter which builds up
on the surface with the annual fall of the leaves. They are also
found growing chiefly in districts where there is chalk or limestone present.

## Soils and Their Preparation

It is not surprising, therefore, that the ideal garden soil has been found to be one that is of a crumb or granular structure, with plenty of pore space through which air circulates, and yet rich in organic matter and its product, humus, and containing calcium carbonate in the form of chalk or lime. A soil that, in horticultural jargon, is called a rich, well-drained, friable loam of only moderate acidity, if any.

Such ideal soils are, in practice, the exception rather than the rule. And fortunately, Clematis will grow in most soils, given good aeration and not too much acidity. Nevertheless, the nearer a soil is to the ideal, the better the plants thrive and perform, and the longer they live. They are unlikely to give good accounts of themselves in soils which soon become arid and dry in summer, or in those which are cold, wet and heavy with much clay and subject to waterlogging in winter.

In preparing a soil for Clematis, the first need is good drainage; the second humus-forming organic matter; and the third lime or chalk to bring it to a level of moderate to slight acidity. In the light of this, we can consider the needs of soils which would benefit from amendment in the interests of finer Clematis.

### CLEMATIS ON SANDY SOILS

Particles of sand are relatively large and coarse. Where they predominate in a soil, they foster large air spaces or pores, and are thus well aerated, and allow also the ready penetration of rain and moisture, and are thus free-draining. They are of a loose texture, in which organic matter oxidises, or burns up, rapidly, and from which soluble mineral salts—the nutrients of plant growth—are easily lost in the drainage waters.

Clematis will usually grow in such soils, unless of pure sand, but with a diminished vigour. And since such soils tend to heat up quickly and become greatly impoverished in drought, life in them for Clematis is precarious in hot summers.

Unless the sub-soil or soil under the top nine inches of soil is impervious clay or rock, there is no need to dig a sandy soil deeply. The chief need is to increase its moisture-holding power.

For serious Clematis gardening, it is of tremendous value to do this first by adding clay to the soil. The clay can be spread on the surface, as well broken as possible, and then forked in. If it can be left to frost action before this is done, it will be found to break into small lumps easily. Clay gives stickiness, moistness and greater plant food resources to a sandy soil. Moreover, it is not readily lost, but exerts its influence for several years. The sandier the soil, the heavier the claying should be, but a rate of one ton of clay to ten to fifteen square yards will make a soil improvement that lasts for up to twenty years.

The second need of a sandy soil is humus-forming organic matter. This can take the form of farmyard manure, composted vegetable refuse, horticultural peat, hop manure, or leaf-mould. In some areas, sewage sludge or dried pulverised sewage is obtainable, and can be used. Forked into the top spit of soil, this material absorbs rain and soil moisture, retaining it at rooting levels in greater quantity. As it rots and forms humus, it not only becomes a colloidal or glue-like material, around each particle of which, sand particles become clumped together in a granule or crumb, but it becomes a source of plant nutrients. With further decomposition, however, the humus breaks up and is lost in the end products or organic decay. As this happens fairly readily in an open soil like sand, it is necessary not only to build up the organic content at the beginning but to replenish it annually.

The third requirement that needs attention is the acid-alkaline balance of the soil. Soil chemists measure this by the hydrogen ion concentration in the soil solution, and express the result in terms of the pH scale. On this scale, pH 7·0 is neutrality. Numbers below 7·0 indicate increasing acidity, and numbers above increasing alkalinity, in geometrical, not arithmetical progression.

In these days, the approximate pH of a soil can be ascertained quite simply with the help of a small soil testing outfit, and the reaction of a sample of the soil to a coloured indicator solution. The gardener can do this himself, and since such soil tests will be helpful to him in other aspects of gardening, the investment of a few shillings in such a tool is well worth while.

Plants differ in their tolerance of pH or soil acidity. In the case of Clematis, the plants will grow in most soils in which the acidity is not too pronounced or not below pH 5·5. But they will grow better in soils of less acidity, preferably of about pH 6·2 to 7·0, and quite well in soils of definite alkalinity where their other essentials are met.

If, therefore, a sandy soil proves to be of an acidity of pH 6·0 or less, it will be beneficial to add acid-neutralising calcium carbonate, preferably in the form of powdered chalk. The amount required would be between six to twelve oz. per sq. yd., according to the degree of acidity. This chalk is added to the surface and raked or pricked in with the fork.

### CLEMATIS ON SILT SOILS

A silt soil is usually composed of sand of various grades down to the finest particles of mineral matter that can remain separate without becoming sticky when wet. It may also contain certain particles of rotted organic matter, and is usually acid in reaction. Such soils are of much closer texture than sand. They are often low-lying and their drainage is determined by the nature of their sub-soil.

In preparing silt soils for Clematis-growing, it is generally necessary to bastard-trench the ground, so that the sub-soil is broken up but kept in place, and the top spit of soil is then turned over on top of the sub-soil. This ensures the Clematis roots being able to penetrate deeply.

Like sandy soils, silts lack structure, and the initial addition of a clay is of similar benefit; but in the case of a silt, the best type of clay is that known as marl. This is a mixture of clay and lime, and helps to offset the acidity of silt, as well as benefiting its structure.

The second need of silt soils is organic matter in a state of active decomposition. Animal manures, hop manures, and well made vegetable compost, are most helpful forked into the top soil as liberally as can be afforded. Then if a soil test reveals undue acidity, a moderate dressing of chalk or lime may be given.

## CLEMATIS ON CLAY SOILS

Clay consists of the powdered and weathered fragments of the oldest rocks. Its particles are not only exceedingly small, the finest of all mineral particles in soil, but plate-like. When wetted, they adhere together like wetted sheets of glass, swelling slightly, becoming sticky, heavy to work, cold, and plastic. If dried, clay holds on to its moisture so tenaciously that it cracks into lumps instead of falling apart like sand, and the lumps often become brick-hard.

Since water moves slowly through clay and its texture is dense, soils containing more than about twenty per cent of clay tend to suffer from poor drainage, coldness especially in spring, and are difficult to cultivate. The more clay a soil contains, the less hospitable it is likely to be for Clematis.

Clematis will, however, grow quite happily in clay soils provided their roots are not waterlogged, and the soils are made more open in texture and provided with lime.

Drainage needs attention first. On soils where the water table rises to flood the top spit in winter, some sub-soil drainage is sure to be necessary. In a border or bed this can usually be provided by a line of four-inch round agricultural tiles laid in a trench about fifteen to eighteen inches deep, with a fall of 1 in 200 to the lower end, where the drain should empty into a ditch, main drain or soakaway. The tiles are packed around with clinker and with a capping of inverted turf, on top of which the soil is replaced.

Clay soils need to be double-dug or bastard-trenched, with the sub-soil being broken up. This sub-soil can also be lightened in texture by having coarse sand, weathered ashes or burnt clay added and forked into it. It is also helpful to add a coarse grade of ground limestone at about 1 lb. per two linear yards of trench. This limestone helps to offset sourness, and will also benefit texture.

The greatest need of a clay soil, however, is humus-forming organic matter, preferably added in a rotted, sponge-dry condition, and finely broken. Rotten animal manure, well-made vegetable compost, hop manure, or horticultural peat can be used, forked in liberally at rates of one to two cwt. per five to seven square yards, and well mixed with the top-soil. It should not be buried deeply under dense, damp earth where it only stagnates inactively.

This material will absorb some of the excess moisture in clay, and also react with the clay particles to form granules or crumbs; thus promoting better aeration, more open pore spaces, and improved drainage.

The organic manuring should be followed by a surface liming of the top soil, using hydrated lime, or ground limestone or chalk. If the soil is prepared in the autumn, it is useful to give basic slag after organic manuring, at six to eight oz. per square yard, and follow with a light liming in the winter.

On the stickiest of clay soils, additional aeration can be provided by making deep V-shaped slits in the soil, and placing doubled straw or reeds upright in the slits, leaving this material to rot in its own good time. The V slits can be made between plants or around planting stations.

Another trick that is useful on cold clay soils is to plant more shallowly and mound the roots and crown above the soil level with good loam. In the case of Clematis this needs care, however, since the roots and the crowns of the plants must not be subject to hot sun, and special attention must be given to shading the roots.

Clay soils are apt to be short of soluble phosphates, and it is always useful to give dressings of bone-meal or basic slag when these soils are being prepared for Clematis.

## Clematis on Chalk

The gardener on chalk or limestone has in the Clematis a genus which will give him ample compensation for his inability to grow Rhododendrons, Azaleas, and other members of the lime-hating family of Ericaceae, for it is overwhelmingly a lime-loving race. This does not mean that Clematis will grow superbly without care, however. They like a soil rich in lime, but they must have their other needs met also.

It is essential to break up the hard sub-soil so that the roots may penetrate deeply. This can be done with a pick or mattock in most instances; though where the sub-soil strata is of rock, it is simpler to have it shattered by exploding small pieces of gelignite under each planting station. It is best to let someone familiar with the handling of explosives do this. A charge that will crack and fissure the rock without displacing it, is sufficient, and need only be done once.

Thereafter, every attention should be given to the top soil, enriching it with organic matter to improve its moisture-retaining capacity. A chalk or limestone soil will assimilate almost any form of organic matter readily, including animal manures, leaves, sewage sludge, hop manure, peat, bark fibre, and weathered sawdust. It is also helpful to mulch the soil regularly during the warm weather months.

# 7

## PLANTING AND AFTER-CARE

*The luxuriant imagination of the painter must be
subjected to the gardener's practical knowledge in
planting, digging and moving earth.*

HUMPHRY REPTON
*Sketches and Hints on Landscape Gardening,* 1795

IN THE life of any perennial garden plant, the moment of planting
—when it is placed in its permanent quarters—is of critical
importance. It is a moment of hiatus, when survival itself is
placed in doubt. And the care and method with which planting
is carried out vitally affect recovery and the whole future performance and well-being of the plant. In the case of Clematis,
this is particularly true. More Clematis are lost through faulty
or inadequate planting than from diseases or pests.

The roots of Clematis are somewhat fleshy. Like other fleshy-
rooted plants, Clematis are apt to find disturbance and transplanting rather trying, and moving them cannot be done with
quite the same freedom as plants having more fibrous and
branching root systems. On no account should the roots be
allowed to become dry when the plant is out of the ground.

### ON BUYING PLANTS

*Caveat emptor*—let the buyer beware—is a maxim of peculiar
significance to the gardener's market when he sets out to buy
plants. As a rule, the gardener has to bide some time before he
can assess the qualities of the plants he buys. Less-than-first-
quality plants are always the most expensive in the long run

both in trouble and in worry. No matter how much care and culture are lavished upon them, they cannot exceed the promise of their youth, and the weak stock, so often offered at cut prices, can never develop satisfactorily. The nurseries which specialize in the raising and growing of Clematis are few. In the interests of continuing goodwill, it pays them to offer only first-class, well-grown plants, and the gardener is wise who places his purchases with them. Many firms offer Clematis, often bought in from elsewhere. There is nothing wrong in this practice, and many such nurserymen are of excellent repute. Nevertheless, it is obviously wiser to buy plants from a grower who has given them continuous routine care, than to buy stock which may have been in a middleman's hands for some time under conditions where they have received only perfunctory attention. The plant that has stood on a shop front for several days, with only a daily watering, is not likely to be in the same condition for planting as one lifted straight from a nursery bed.

Apart from ensuring that plants are in healthy, good condition, the gardener should insist on his Clematis being (1) grown on their own roots; (2) pot-grown; and (3) young in age.

Choice hybrids and varieties may be grafted on to rootstocks of *Clematis viticella*, a practice which permits rapid increase in their numbers. Unfortunately, such grafted plants often die suddenly, and appear to be more susceptible to the parasitic pests and fungi apt to attack young plants. For permanent plants it is far better to have plants growing on their own roots. The best firms now send out their plants on their own roots, and these can be ordered from them with perfect trust.

It is quite practical to transplant Clematis from the open ground, provided the roots are not allowed to dry out, and the plants are moved expeditiously and correctly. When plants have to come from nurseries afar, and spend several days in transit, however, it is far better to buy young pot-grown stock. It travels better. It is easier to plant. It prospers without much setback due to shock, as the roots remain largely undisturbed in their soil. It can be planted at almost any time of the year.

*Clematis montana* tumbling over a low wall.

Clematis Marie Boisselot. Has a beautifully formed flower, white with eight sepals.
Flowers in May-June and again in September-October. A vigorous grower.

Pot-grown stock should, however, be young; otherwise, the roots may become entwined and pot-bound, and the chances of such a plant making a fine specimen are fewer. Moreover, young plants are the more vigorous in establishing themselves, and are more likely to give of their full quality in subsequent growth.

## TIME FOR PLANTING

Clematis in pots may be planted at any time of the year when the weather serves, and the soil is in a suitable workable condition. It would be unwise to plant in a summer drought, however, or when the soil is waterlogged or frozen. The best time for planting is early autumn, from the last week of September to the end of November; especially on light soils. If the soil is heavy and subject to waterlogging in winter, spring planting in March is probably safer. On well-drained loam soils, however, it is practical to plant at any time between September and March when the weather is mild and the soil free and workable.

In planting Clematis which have been raised in open ground, early autumn or spring are the most favourable times; though if planting stations are well prepared, plants can be moved under mild conditions during the winter. Great care is needed, however, to lift the plants with their root systems as intact as possible.

No matter how well it is done, the planting of either a pot-grown or an open-ground-grown Clematis causes some shock to growth, and the need for some adjustment to its new environment by the plant. As evergreens find it difficult to re-establish themselves when moved in winter, it is best to plant the evergreen Clematis in early autumn or spring.

## PREPARING PLANTING STATIONS

Trouble taken in preparing the individual planting stations for Clematis is repaid in the early recovery of the plants from the shock of transplanting and their subsequent good growth.

A planting hole or station at least eighteen inches across is needed, from which the top spit of about nine inches should be removed and placed on one side, while the sub-soil is broken up. A heavy sub-soil should be lightened by forking in coarse sand, and, if acid, a dressing of ground limestone or chalk at about one lb. per sq. yd. A light sub-soil can be improved by forking in three or four bucketfuls of well broken clay or marl. The bottom of the planting station should then be firmed and finished as a shallow concave mound.

If planting is contemplated in ground subject to water-logging in winter, some way of draining excess water away from the roots will have to be found. A layer of clinker and ash, or broken brick and rubble, four to five inches thick, under fifteen inches of soil, is helpful. It should be given a concave shape so that the water drains away from the planting station rather than towards it.

The top-soil may then be balanced to suit the plants. If it is of a good loam character with a crumb structure, little need be added to it beyond a dressing of superphosphate at one oz. per square yard, or bone-meal at three oz. per square yard. Rich fertilisation at the outset is undesirable, as the chief object of the planter is to get his plants to settle down and establish good rooting.

A heavy soil should be lightened by adding thoroughly well-rotted organic matter (leaf-mould, decayed manure or compost) to it, and coarse sand. A light top-soil will benefit also from the addition of rotted organic material, or moist peat, and well-broken clay or marl. A phosphatic fertiliser is helpful to stimulate root action. Bone-meal at 3 oz. per square yard can be used in autumn planting, but superphosphate at one oz. or bone flour at two oz. per square yard is more useful in late winter or spring.

## How to Plant

A Clematis plant should be set so that the crown of its roots is about two inches below the levelled surface of the soil. A plant moved from the open ground should have its roots carefully spread and spaced over the concave base of the planting station, so that no root is cramped or bent. A little soil should then be sifted in to cover the roots, and worked with the fingers to firm contact with the roots, leaving no air pockets. Then more soil can be added and firmed, until the station is filled up. A final firming of the soil can be given by treading with the feet, but concrete firmness is not desired, as too much pressure can easily break the fleshy roots. The filled planting hole should then be soaked with water, and when this water has drained into the soil, a light mulch of rotted organic litter can be added.

Plants bought-in from good nurseries will be, or should be in pots. They will be young and provided with a cane to which the stems will be fastened. An unfortunate practice is growing of sending out Clematis wrapped only in polythene sheets and a little soil. This may cheapen the price, but little soil remains intimately connected with the roots after transit and such plants often fail to recover well after transplanting, if at all.

After unwrapping a Clematis in its pot as received from the nursery, it is a good plan to let the pot soak in a bucket of water for a few hours before planting. The stem will be tied to a cane, and should not be disturbed. The plant can be readily taken out of its pot by inverting it, and with the fingers of one hand spread over the top, tapping it on the edge of a wooden bench or spade handle, or by carefully pushing through the drainage hole at the bottom with the flat end of a pencil, wooden skewer or stick.

Without disturbing the soil ball more than can be avoided, any roots which are twisted or wrapped round the outside or base of the soil ball should be carefully loosened, disentangled and straightened to their full length, using a pointed stick. Care is needed as they break easily, but kinked and bent roots cannot straighten themselves, and kinks and twists restrict and stunt future growth.

With the outer roots straightened, the plant can be set in the planting hole, and soil sifted around them evenly spaced on the mounded base of the hole. When these roots have been firmed in soil, the hole can be filled, firmed and watered. If the soil is very heavy, a high proportion of sand can be mixed with the first sifting over the roots.

## WHERE TO PLANT

The natural desire for all climbing Clematis is to have their roots in the shade and their foliage and flowers in the sun. In planting, therefore, the roots should be settled, when possible, on the shaded side of the supports they are to climb. Shade encourages the development of a crowded network of roots near the surface which can feed on the richest soil. Plants on posts or tripods soon develop a head or canopy of foliage that provides good shade for their roots. But where plants are placed in the open it is always wise to mulch the rooting area with organic litter to preserve a cool, moist surface root run.

When plants must be set where their roots are subject to the direct rays of the sun, it is a good thing to arrange shade to be cast by plants at their feet. For the first year or so annuals can be sown; later, shrubs like *Erica carnea* and its varieties, *Cotoneaster congesta, Cotoneaster dammeri,* dwarf Lavenders, *Vinca minor,* Dwarf Veronicas, and Helianthemums can be grown to give the required shade.

When planting Clematis on walls, it is better to plant with the crown well removed from the structure. Walls are apt to dry out the soil near them with surprising rapidity, and since Clematis need ample moisture, the plants are likely to do better when set a little away from the walls they adorn, with the stems trained at a slight slope towards them.

Clematis are well able to hold their own in competition with supporting shrubs or trees when fully established. When planting, however, a good planting station should be made, and the roots mulched regularly.

## THE AFTER-CARE OF NEWLY PLANTED CLEMATIS

No pruning of autumn- or winter-planted Clematis should be done until February or March. At this time, when it is seen that the buds are just beginning to move and show green, the stems should be shortened to just above a node showing living buds about six to twelve inches above the base of the plant. Plants planted in spring or summer should be pruned back in the same way, once it is seen that they have recovered from the setback of being transplanted. It is a common mistake to prune plants severely immediately after planting, whereas they establish themselves more readily when the growth they have is left intact until new root hairs have formed.

Great care should be taken of the short stem left after pruning. It is best tied securely but loosely to a cane or stake leaning towards the support up which the plant is to grow, in order that it does not kink nor become weakened by being blown about. Its position should be well marked so that there is no likelihood of its being cut or injured by hoeing. Slugs and snails are fond of young Clematis and can rasp the bark off young stems to kill plants overnight. Protection from this danger can be given by applying a soil molluscide based on metaldehyde to the rooting area after planting, and renewing as warranted.

Newly planted Clematis do not need any rich feeding during their first year. They need water constantly, however, and in dry weather should be watered and syringed, especially in spring, when the cold and drying easterly winds are apt to blow.

When properly planted, the plants grow with vigour, but the first year should be devoted primarily to fostering and training the initial framework of branches. The tips of new shoots should be pinched out between finger and thumb nail in late spring, when soft and tender, and again in summer, to induce the branching which gives a plant well furnished with growth from near the base. Plants on walls and fences, in particular, need to have their first branches trained and spaced to form a framework that allows the maximum of wall space to be covered and clothed with flowers without shoots intertangling.

Mulching is generally necessary for all plants in their first year, to conserve moisture in the soil, to keep the roots cool, and to feed the plants. It is best to use well-rotted, moist organic matter, like decayed manure, good vegetable compost, moist peat or leaf-mould, and apply after rain. The mulch should cover the rooting area but only to within about six inches of the base of the plant. This part should be left open to absorb rain and water. By the end of the growing season, much of the mulch can be lightly forked into the top two inches of soil.

Some gardeners place a thin layer of coal ashes from the fire immediately around the base of Clematis, and this helps to deter slugs and snails without hindering the penetration of rain or water. Once well-established, the matured stems and fibrous bark are less attractive to slugs and snails, and only young foliage and shoots may need protection. This can be given by spraying with a suspension solution of Metaldehyde, when the ubiquitous garden molluscs are noted to be active.

In subsequent years, the established Clematis lay no very great burden upon the gardener's time, labour or skill. Routine care becomes largely a matter of controlling weeds, manuring, watering, feeding and pruning.

Most weeds can be dealt with in the normal routine garden weeding, but climbing weeds such as Bindweed (*Convolvulus spp.*) may become a nuisance if allowed to get hold. Such weeds can be eradicated, however, by painting their foliage with one of selective weed-killers based on 2,4-D or 2,4,5-T, or immersing their growing tips in a jar half-filled with the weed-killer solution for a few hours or overnight. So long as the solution does not come into contact with the Clematis, the weeds succumb without the Clematis being harmed.

Clematis are often planted and forgotten—left to do their best on their own. Nevertheless, the prodigious production of stem, leaf and flower of which some of the large-flowered Clematis are capable deserves encouragement by some system of regular manuring and feeding. On good soils it is often sufficient to give an annual topdressing of rotted manure or compost in the spring, and then in autumn when the remains of this mulch is pricked into the soil, give four oz. of bone-meal per square yard. On heavy soils, it may be necessary to supplement the organic topdressing with one of lime every fourth year, or to add lime-mortar rubble, in the autumn.

Clematis will almost certainly respond better in light soils if given a complete fertiliser, say one of two parts by weight hoof and horn meal, two parts superphosphate, and one part sulphate of potash at four oz. per square yard, before applying the annual mulch of organic matter. On acid sands, lime should be given in the form of ground chalk or lime mortar rubble every fourth year.

Water is a constant need when the plants are making active growth. While regular mulching increases the water-retentive capacity of the soil, it is always helpful to flood the rooting area of plants periodically when dry spells are prolonged, especially in the case of plants growing on walls.

Many Clematis, particularly the large-flowered hybrids, benefit from a feeding of liquid manure at two-week intervals during flowering. This can consist of the dilute straw-coloured liquor drawn from a butt in which a sack of rotted dung has been immersed, or a solution of $\frac{1}{2}$ oz. Chilean potash nitrate per gallon of water, or a proprietary liquid fertiliser solution.

Finally, by mastering and applying the art of pruning Clematis, the full glory of the genus can be realised, and this is of sufficient importance to merit a separate chapter.

# 8

## THE PRUNING OF CLEMATIS

*Superfluous branches*
*We lop away, that bearing boughs may live.*

WM. SHAKESPEARE
*Richard II*, III, *iv*, 51

T HE ART of pruning may be defined as the regulation of the
growth of a plant by the cutting away of parts of it in order to
enhance its performance in the eye of the cultivator. In the
case of Clematis, the aims of the pruner are to so shape the
plant that it can make the fullest and best use of the space
available for it, and to improve its flowering display. At the
same time, pruning has the effect of admitting more air and
light to the plant and its parts to keep it healthy and to mature
its shoots more satisfactorily.

Left to grow naturally, Clematis soon become masses of
tangled shoots of disappointing shape, especially on the artificial
supports so often provided for them in the garden. By disciplining their growth and thinning out shoots, more shapely
plants capable of more prolonged and better flowering are
obtained.

It is sometimes said that pruning is unnatural and therefore
to be decried. In fact, Nature has her precedents. Shrubs and
trees are always being pruned by wind and weather, even by
parasitic infection or infestation, whereby parts of a plant die
back and the stronger and more healthy parts survive. The
ageing of growth is in many respects a pruning, for the older
wood tends to become less vigorous and less productive of
flowers and fruits, and its place is taken by younger and more

virile shoots. What Nature does at random, however, the gardener attempts with greater system.

The removal of shoot growth from a plant like the Clematis not only removes plant tissue, but also substances such as food reserves in the tissues, which would otherwise have been used for growth. It is a minor shock to the whole economy of the plant and has reflex repercussions on the root system. The plant reacts by making new growth in due season, and the more that has been cut away, the more vigorous the reaction and the greater the amount of new growth, other things being equal.

The strength of the new growth flows to the youngest parts of the plant remaining, and is expressed most vigorously through the youngest or topmost buds, as a rule. To induce growth to break low down beyond a pruning cut, it is necessary to divert the sap flow into lower buds either by bending the stem or interrupting it by simple knife cuts or nicks above the buds to be forced into growth.

Since the sap stream will only flow into tissues from which new growth is initiated, such as buds, it is important when pruning to make cuts immediately above the nodes, or at the base or junction of one shoot with another. A cut between nodes means a stub or snag above the buds into which the sap ceases to flow, and it dies back, possibly becoming a point of entry for disease.

After planting, new Clematis have their stems cut back to within six to twelve inches of the ground, just above live buds showing green, in February or March. In the subsequent growing season, vigorous shoot growth will be made, which should be trained to the supports and to occupy the space where the shoots are to flower. This is particularly important in the case of Clematis on walls, fences or flat surfaces; the shoots which are to form the main branches being trained out separately and spread so that they do not become a tangle.

The general principles that govern the pruning of shrubs apply also to Clematis; namely that those plants which flower on the growths made during the previous year, and which flower in the early part of the year, are pruned *after* flowering;

while those which flower on the new growth of the current year and from July onwards are pruned, if desired, in early spring. These principles apply with certain refinements in individual cases.

## PRUNING THE EARLY-FLOWERING CLEMATIS

The Clematis which flower between January and June, bud and bloom from shoots grown during the previous year, which are left intact until the current year's blossoming is over. In order to prune these early-flowering kinds correctly, however, it is necessary to divide them into two sub-divisions.

The first sub-division consists of the Clematis which produce their flowers directly from the growths made in the previous year. It includes Clematis of the *alpina, montana,* and *armandii* groups, and the species *C. chrysocoma.* When these plants are grown on a wall, fence or trellis with the purpose of covering its surface, some sacrifice of flowering must be made in the interests of establishing a framework of branches. Thus, in the second year after planting, the branch growths should be cut back to within twenty-four to thirty inches of their base in February; and the following February, the new growths should again be cut back though less severely, say to within six to eight feet of their base. These branches, properly tied in, should then ensure growth that will furnish flowers over the whole space allotted to the plants.

Their regular pruning, after the initial training, is done immediately after flowering, as required to keep them to the space given to them. Where they have ample room for expansion, little pruning will be necessary, except for the removal of surplus shoots. When it is desired to restrict them within limited space, the old wood which has flowered may be cut out as required, and the new young shoots when they break may be trained in to bear the next year's flowers. When these plants are allowed to grow unchecked, growth is apt to become a tangle, and in such instances, it is feasible to thin out the growths of the *alpina* and *montana* groups, while the evergreen *armandii* group may be thinned in February.

## The Pruning of Clematis

The second sub-division consists of the Clematis which produce their flowers on short growths from the shoots made in the previous year. It includes the varieties and hybrids of the *florida* and *patens* groups, which flower in May-June, but which may also bloom again in September and October. When grown on walls or where growth must be kept within bounds, and once the initial framework has been established, pruning consists first of cutting out all dead and weak shoots in late January or February when the buds begin to swell, and retaining only strong shoots for flowering, which are tied in. They may be shortened a little but not more than by about one-fourth their length. Secondly, as soon as flowering is over, the old shoots may be pruned back severely, and about half of the flowered shoots can be treated in this way. New shoots will break and these should be tied in as soon as possible to mature and flower next year. When two strong shoots arise from the same node on a branch, it is wise to prune one out, and throw all the growth energy into the other.

### Pruning the Summer-flowering Clematis

The Clematis which bloom from July onwards flower from the leaf axils or the ends of shoots of the current season's growth. They include Clematis of the *jackmanii, lanuginosa, viticella,* and *texensis* groups, and late-flowering species, such as *C. grata, C. x jouiniana, C. orientalis, C. paniculata,* and *C. vitalba.*

When it is found desirable to prune these plants, the work should be done in early spring, as soon as the buds begin to swell. The way in which they are pruned depends upon the use being made of the plants.

The large-flowering hybrids of the *jackmanii, lanuginosa* and *viticella* groups, for instance, when grown on low walls, balustrades, fences, trellis, and where it is necessary to keep them within a limited space, may be pruned by cutting really hard back to within two to four feet of the ground each spring.

Where they are grown to fill larger spaces, or to flower rather high up, the plants must first be trained to make a framework of branches, which are stopped at the height from which

75

new young shoots are needed to break each year. Subsequent pruning then consists simply of cutting back these annual shoots to suitably placed strong buds each spring, about four to six inches from the base of their growth.

These methods of pruning not only enable a greater space to be covered with bloom, but keep the plants well furnished with flowering growth.

In the case of the *lanuginosa* group, however, flowering can be promoted earlier in many cases, since some varieties will flower from old as well as young wood. The plants of this group, when early flowering is desired, can be pruned in the same way as the spring flowering kinds; the shoots being thinned, or a proportion being cut back only, and others tied in and left to bear early flowers. Hybrids such as "Beauty of Worcester", "Miriam Markham", "Proteus", which produce double and single flowers on old and young wood respectively, are well worth treating in this way; others are "Lady North-cliffe", "Lord Neville", "Marie Boisselot", "Mrs. Cholmondeley", and "William Kennett".

The summer-flowering species such as *C. campaniflora, C. flammula, C. grata, C.* x *jouiniana, C. orientalis, C. paniculata, C. rehderiana, C. tangutica* and its varieties, *C. vitalba* and *C. viticella* and its small-flowered hybrids may all be pruned by cutting the previous year's growth severely back to a suitable node within a few inches of its base.

The hybrids of the *texensis* group are a little tender, and some growths may die back partially each winter. They may be pruned in early spring by cutting the previous year's growth back to base or to a convenient node.

Pruning, by disciplining the growth of Clematis, enables us to tailor plants to fit allotted space, and with a modicum of training, to make the most of their superb ornamental quality and floral colour. It is especially rewarding in the case of the large- and small-flowered hybrids grown on flat surfaces like walls, where the thinning of shoots and the periodical cutting back of growth, keeps up a constant regeneration of young wood endowed with flowering vigour.

It must, however, be borne in mind that pruning is not just

a mechanical artifice, and the guiding principles here laid down are not rigid and absolute. To get the finest results from pruning, the gardener must anticipate the reactions of the plant to restriction. Hard or severe pruning stimulates a strong reaction and vigorous shoot growth. Light pruning is followed by either light to moderate shoot growth, or greater flowering vigour on the part of the pruned shoot if done before flowering, or a maturing of the pruned shoot with the ripening of its wood and good bud development for the following year, if the pruning is done late.

By studying and observing the individuality of his plants and their reactions, the gardener can exercise his pruning skill to greater effect in securing the results he desires.

Regular annual pruning, however, requires the complement of regular feeding. Each time growth is removed, we are taking away substances which the plant has had to draw from the soil, and deplete its fertility to that extent. Moreover, pruning forces the plant to make new growth which itself requires the support of a fertile soil. Consequently, pruned plants need feeding more than unpruned.

The emphasis laid on pruning in this chapter does not mean that Clematis will not succeed without it. It simply means that they are likely to give a much more pleasing garden display, and can be more effectively kept in bounds. Nevertheless, there is not the same need for pruning where plants are grown informally, such as where they are planted to scramble through trees or large bushes, or to cover or drape rocks. An occasional inspection and a removal of older wood to stimulate young renewal growth are the chief needs under such conditions.

# 9

## CLEMATIS IN POTS

*There is no spot of ground, however arid, bare,*
*or ugly, that cannot be tamed into such a state as*
*may give an impression of beauty and delight.*

GERTRUDE JEKYLL
*Home and Garden,* 1900

THE GROWING of flowering plants in pots, tubs, earthenware, stone, or concrete vases, is a pleasant and rewarding one.

It makes it possible for many to enjoy the delights of gardening where soil resources are limited, such as in backyards
concreted or asphalted over, or in roof gardens. It gives us
plants which can be moved and placed where they can be most
effective to dispel the drab ugliness of walls, to soften the harsh
aridity of concrete, or to clothe the bareness of empty or waste
garden space.

For these purposes, the decorative grace and floral beauty
of the Clematis are unsurpassable, but unfortunately often
neglected or ignored. Yet there is no better way for those who
want to make the most of the Clematis genus within the limits
of a small garden than to grow some of the finer varieties and
hybrids in pots.

Clematis growing in their own containers can be put to a
variety of uses. As they come into flower, they can grace walls,
lend distinction to paved terraces or walks. They are excellent
for forecourts, and can be placed very effectively on either side
of a porch, the entrance doorway, or at the foot of a stairway.
They can be placed at the foot of pillars or trellises up which
their growth can be trained. They make excellent plants for
the conservatory or cold greenhouse.

# Clematis in Pots

## CLEMATIS FOR POT CULTURE

The roots of Clematis range far, deep and wide when planted in the soil out of doors. Confinement in a pot checks their range, and to some extent this also inhibits the top growth in stature. Whereas there is no limit to the kind of garden Clematis that can be grown in a pot which is to remain permanently where it is placed, it is better to grow the rather less vigorous kinds in pots that will be moved from time to time.

One of the advantages of pot culture is that it allows us to grow the more tender, very early flowering Clematis which can then be moved into sheltered corners where winter frost or inclemancy cannot damage the blossoms. The evergreen Fern-leaved *Clematis calycina*, for instance, bears its yellow-white, bell-like flowers, spotted reddish-purple, against shining, bronzy-purple foliage, during November to February when other flowers are few; and *C. cirrhosa* is also evergreen and of winter-flowering habit, putting out creamy-greenish white, hanging flowers, quite freely during January to March.

The New Zealand species, *C. afoliata*, which is known as the Rush-stemmed Clematis from its peculiar habit of producing drooping, rush-like green shoots or very slender twigs, with almost no leaves, and bears cascades of deliciously scented, small whitish-green flowers in May, and *C. indivisa*, an evergreen, with white flowers in panicles in May and June, are only sufficiently hardy for all the year round out of doors in south-western counties, and can best be grown in pots elsewhere.

The spring-flowering *C. alpina* and its several forms is most useful, since plants can be moved in their pots to where their flowering will be valued. *C. macropetala* and its var. *markhamii* with their hanging flowers of papery pointed petals make charming subjects for pots. *C. montana* and its varieties and *C. spooneri* are somewhat vigorous, but not averse to being pot-grown. To these various species, we can add the large-flowered hybrids of *C. x jackmanii*, *C. lanuginosa*, *C. florida*, *C. patens* and *C. vitella* to bloom in the summer and early autumn months.

Plants to be grown in pots may be raised from seeds, from cuttings, from layers or as grafted plants (*see Chapter 14*), or bought as pot-grown specimens, which are usually supplied in 4½-inch pots. Home-grown seedling plants will usually be potted up into 4½-inch pots in their second year. From 4½-inch pots the plants may be transferred to 8½-inch or 9½-inch pots (twenty-fours or sixteens) in October or the following March. In these pots, the plants can be relied upon to make good growth and develop into fine flowering specimens.

Plants in pots need careful planting, since the pots become their more-or-less permanent quarters. There must be good drainage, and the bottom of the pot should be covered with an inch layer of broken crocks, with an inverted large crock over the drainage hole to prevent its becoming choked. On top of the crocks, a thin layer of beech or oak leaves is placed to prevent soil washing down into the crocks and clogging their air space.

When a plant is taken out of its 4½-inch pot, the roots at the base may be disentangled, but the soil ball left intact. This is placed in the new large pot so that it remains at the same soil level after potting. The plant is potted with moderate firmness into a fresh soil compost.

This compost needs to be porous and well-aerated, and yet retentive of moisture. Gardeners of the old school preferred a mixture of two or three parts by bulk of chopped turfy fibrous loam (the smaller quantity if heavy and clayey), one part each well-rotted beech or oak leaf-mould, and one part coarse sand; to which was added one 3-inch pot-full each of bone-meal, wood ash, and lime rubble (or ground chalk). Such a compost will still give satisfactory results, but the modern gardener will probably find some ingredients hard to come by, and by adopting the scientifically standardised John Innes Potting Compost can eliminate any guesswork.

The John Innes Potting Compost suitable for Clematis in their final potting is:

> 7 parts by volume of medium loam, preferably sterilised.
>
> 3 parts by volume of granulated sedge or moss peat.

*ematis tangutica*. This is a fast growing climber and often reaches 16 feet. Butter
llow flowers. Late June-October.

*Clematis montana rubens.* When young this variety has purple leaves. Flowers are pinky-mauve and it flowers in May.

Double Clematis. A beautiful specimen for growing up pillars and pergolas.

2 parts by volume of coarse sharp sand.

*Plus*

2½ oz. ground limestone or chalk.

12 oz. John Innes Base Fertiliser (consisting of 2 parts by weight hoof and horn meal, 2 parts by weight superphosphate, 1 part by weight sulphate of potash).

The peat should be moist, and the whole compost thoroughly mixed so that the ingredients are evenly distributed.

A further refinement, whatever compost is used, is to add some horticultural vermiculite, up to 25 per cent by bulk. This micaceous material is inert in itself, but in its exfoliated state can retain up to almost six times its own weight in water while remaining well aerated. It thus helps to maintain physical conditions in pots that are conducive to steady growth.

In potting, soil compost should be placed over the crocks and a thin layer of leaf-mould, and firmed, without ramming solid, to the level necessary to take the soil ball of the transplant. Soil compost is then sifted in all around and firmed, and planting should finish with the soil level about one inch below the pot rim. This allows for watering and top-dressing.

A stake should be inserted during potting, and when completed two further stakes can be added with cross-piece to form a lattice up which growths may be trained. These stakes should be five to six feet tall.

Such plants in large pots can be kept in a sheltered part of the garden on a bed of ashes during the winter and when they are not in flower, and be moved into position by walls, posts, entrances or where their beauty and colour can be best displayed when they come into bud. Bearing in mind the need of the roots for a cool rotting medium, however, it is best to place the pots inside another container, such as a larger pot, concrete jar or vase or tub, filling the space between with horticultural vermiculite. If this is kept moist, the plants will thrive through the driest drought, and watering anxieties can be forgotten.

When plants are to be grown in permanent positions, they can be planted in large ornamental earthenware or clay vases, concrete receptacles, or wooden boxes or tubs, preferably of teak or rot-resistant red cedar. If a less durable wood is used, it should be treated with a suitable wood preservative such as a cuprous compound—not with creosote which is injurious to plants. Planting should be done with the same care as in large pots, with particular attention to good drainage.

It is an effective plan to grow Clematis in wooden boxes, tubs or barrels where the native soil is uncongenial to the genus, or on acid soils where califuge plants are to be grown nearby. The containers can be sunk to near soil level where the Clematis are to grow.

A well-planted Clematis can be grown successfully for several years in its container. As the plants develop each year, they need regular watering during the growing season, and when buds form, they benefit from being given diluted liquid manure or a foliar spraying with a nutrient solution about once weekly, until they come into flower. Then feeding should be suspended, though watering is still necessary in warm weather.

When flowering is over and the plants become dormant, watering can be reduced, and if the plants remain out of doors all the year round, no winter watering is necessary. During the dormant period, the top inch or two of soil in the containers should be loosened and removed, and replaced with fresh soil compost. In the case of plants in pots, the plants can be turned out, and a little of the old soil removed at the base and sides to be replaced with fresh compost. A plant that has outgrown its pot can be potted on to a larger size. This work can be done best in October-November or March.

# IO

## CLEMATIS UNDER GLASS

*It always seems to me that one of the things most worth doing about a garden is to try to make every part of it beautiful.*

GERTRUDE JEKYLL
*Home and Garden,* 1900

IT IS extraordinary how so beautiful and so floriferous a genus as Clematis is neglected as a source of interest and enjoyment under glass. You can look in vain for any word of guidance in the modern gardening books. Even the omniscience of the *Dictionary of Gardening,* sponsored by the ultimate authority, The Royal Horticultural Society, falls down on this point. Nevertheless, the genus furnishes exceptionally fine climbers that can be used to add distinction and beauty to the cold and cool greenhouse, or conservatory.

Under the protection of glass a Clematis unfolds its flowers in full perfection, completely unmarred by rain and untorn by wind, and remains one of the most pest and disease-free climbers in cultivation. Plants can be on hardwood or wire trellis close to the wall of a lean-to structure, becoming a sheet of colour when in bloom. They are equally adaptable twining up the support pillars or posts in the full-span greenhouse, or can be grown from one end, preferably the northerly end, and trained along rafters, from which drooping shoots can show their flowers in cascades of colour.

Of the hardy Clematis with which we are concerned here, none of them require heat. All of them are satisfactory in the cool or cold greenhouse, and even for the encouragement of earlier bloom, need no more than a maximum night temperature of about 55° F. Only on the coldest of winter nights is it vital to furnish heat or protection, and then only for the least hardy kinds in the more exposed localities.

One of the finer ornamental species welcoming the shelter of glass is the New Zealand *Clematis indivisa*, a beautiful and vigorous evergreen with tri-foliate, blunt-ended leaves, producing starry flowers with six to eight sepals of the purest white, in panicles freely from the leaf axils, in April-May. The plant is unisexual, and the flowers in the female are about two inches across. In the male, they are up to three inches across, and the presence of yellow stamens with pink anthers in the centre, add to their beauty. In the variety *lobata*, the leaflets are lobed or coarsely toothed, and the flowers somewhat larger.

These New Zealanders are only hardy enough for mild maritime gardens along the south-west coast of Britain to be planted out of doors in their youth, but they grow strongly, and when a plant has overcrowded its greenhouse space and made some older hard wood, it might well be tried on a sheltered wall outside.

The greenhouse is also a rightful place for the winter-flowering *C. calycina*, with its decorative, deeply cut fern-like leaflets, turning a bronzy-purple in winter, and producing four-sepalled, yellowish-white, bell-shaped flowers, spotted red, singly from the leaf axils. They are not showy, but are very welcome in their appearance through the winter from November to February. The whole plant has a slender elegance and grows twelve to fifteen feet when unchecked.

*C. cirrhosa* is a somewhat similar pretty, rather than spectacular, winter-flowering evergreen, with smaller ovate and glabrous leaves, and creamy-white nodding flowers of similar character produced rather later, from January to March. The whole plant is more dwarf, not exceeding ten feet, but has the reputation of being hardier than *C. calycina*.

Another early flowering evergreen worth seeking for the cool greenhouse is *C. napaulensis*, growing with vigour from twenty to thirty feet; its leaves tri- to quin-foliate, with lance-shaped leaflets of two to three inches in length, and curious, small, creamy-yellow, four-sepalled flowers with central clusters of purple stamens, borne in single-stalked clusters of eight or ten, from the leaf axils early in the New Year into spring. In south-western counties, it can be planted out on a sheltered wall.

The spring-flowering species and hybrids provide some of the finest early bloom for greenhouses. The Chinese *C. armandii* grows with vigour and its white four- to six-sepalled flowers, up to 2½ inches across, are fragrant and are produced in axillary clusters in April and May, and its dark, glossy green, somewhat large trifoliate leaves are attractive the year round. In var. "Apple Blossom", the flowers are pink tinged and the leaves bronzy-green, while var. "Snowdrift", with pure white flowers, has the largest, leathery, glossy green leaves.

*C. meyeniana* is another Chinese species on a par with the *C. armandii* group for its display of white bloom in large, loose, hanging panicles of four-sepalled small flowers, sweetly scented but smaller, and evergreen leathery leaves that are entire, smaller and narrower. This plant is well worth growing, for it blooms in February and March unsparingly.

A rather cool environment is preferred by the hardy *C. alpina* and its varieties, growing six to eight feet high, and this deciduous group can be well adapted to the cooler part of a cold greenhouse, where it will produce its small, nodding, four-sepalled, blue, bell-like flowers from early April. "Columbine", lavender-blue, "Ruby", rosy-red, and "White Moth", double white, are distinctive forms.

For May flowering, the deciduous, slender *C. macropetala*, with its azure-blue, pointed sepalled, large flowers, or its clear pink var. *markhamii*, can be grown with confidence; and the somewhat tender New Zealand rush-stemmed, *C. afoliata*, which grows only to six feet, may be given room for its daphne-scented clusters of greenish-white small flowers.

The hybrid *C. x vedrariensis* is a choice plant of French breeding which does not require too much space, and repays for its greenhouse culture with flowers of a delicate rose-pink, up to two inches across, on long, slender hairy stalks. May is also the month when the deciduous Bell Rue of North America, *C.*

*verticilliaris*, puts out its four-sepalled, purple-blue flowers singly on three-inch stalks from the joints of the previous year's shoots, but it is rare, and is best grown from seed.

As spring merges into summer, the range of choice widens. Taking first the species, however, which are of some botanical as well as decorative interest, one of the finest for under glass is the Chinese *C. florida*, which tries to remain evergreen in mild winters, but commands attention when its large, single, creamy-white, oval-sepalled flowers come in bloom. Those of its var. *sieboldii* are the more striking for a central cluster of deep purple stamenoides. Growth reaches eight to twelve feet.

*C. pavoliniana* is a Chinese evergreen, resembling *C. armandii*, growing to fifteen feet, with glossy, narrow ovate foliage, and clusters of 1 ½ inch wide, pure white flowers in clusters of four to seven, delightfully scented, in June. Its compatriot, *C. chrysocoma*, is deciduous, and may be confined to six or eight feet tall, producing its pink-tinged, white flowers freely on long stalks from late June onwards into autumn.

The deciduous Japanese *C. patens*, growing up to twelve feet, has long, pointed, entire, leafleted foliage, to offset its solitary, spreading, six- to eight-sepalled, light to deep blue flowers, measuring some four to six inches across, in June, and it is, of course, a parent of several singularly fine large-flowered hybrids, which usher in the summer season of Clematis bloom. Among them may be mentioned "Edouard Desfosse", with extremely large violet-mauve flowers, and "Nelly Moser", pale mauve-pink with a deep carmine bar.

Throughout the summer, the large-flowered hybrids of *C. florida*, *C. x jackmanii* and *C. lanuginosa* will bear their fine, beautifully disposed, elegant, large flowers for us in the cold greenhouse, only asking for ample ventilation, moist, cool conditions for their roots, and some shade on the more torrid odd days.

A great deal of joy can be gained from the yellow flowering species, particularly *C. tangutica*, which bears its nodding, four-sepalled rich yellow, slender-pointed flowers on their long stalks from July onwards, to be joined by silky heads of ripening seeds later in the year. The best form is "Gravetye" variety.

*C. serratifolia* is a somewhat similar slender deciduous climber, with its leaves much cut, and bears soft yellow smaller flowers in ones to threes in late summer, which are followed by silky seed heads. Of the same season comes *C. orientalis*, with deciduous pinnate foliage, bearing yellow flowers, $1\frac{1}{2}$ to 2 inches across, with their four sepals reflexing, and giving a delightful fragrance, with masses of silky seed heads following in late autumn. All these plants grow quite vigorously when settled, and need severe pruning to prevent them becoming an uncontrolled tangle.

When grown out of doors, the Japanese *C. paniculata* often flowers too late to develop and fulfil its promise. It needs a hot summer to bring the full flowering of its panicles of hawthorn-scented, pure-white flowers, and subsequent feathery seed heads. Obviously, it will have a happier chance of flowering with its full beauty in September within a greenhouse.

Lovers of fragrance should not miss the hybrid *C.* x *rubro-marginata*, a deciduous climber growing to twelve feet, bearing masses of small white flowers, with six sepals marked reddish-violet towards the margins, and diffusing a scent that is rich and refreshing. Seed heads are formed which take on a pleasing reddish-brown sheen on a sunny autumn day.

For bloom in late summer and autumn, the hybrid forms of *C. viticella* and its varieties are a source of colour and fragrance. Coming from Southern Europe, the species appreciates the winter protection of glass, and will grow to twelve feet and more, producing flowers abundantly in shades of purply-blue, or blue, lavender or rosy-purple, measuring $1\frac{1}{2}$ to 2 inches across. *Albiflora* is a splendid white variety, *kermesiana* flowers an intense vinous red, *coerulea*, blue-violet, and *flore-pleno* has double flowers. It is, however, among the larger flowered hybrids that the finest show will be found; the bright blue *ascotiensis*; the petunia red "Ernest Markham"; the translucent white, with mauve-pink bar, "Huldine"; the rich deep purple "Royal Velours"; and the bright carmine-red "Ville de Lyon".

One other interesting and beautiful group of summer flowering Clematis consists of the North American *C. texensis* and its hybrids. The species is difficult to obtain and rather tender, but produces nodding bell-shaped flowers of red or scarlet on long slender stalks freely, and has pinnate foliage with glaucous, entire, roundish to ovate leaflets. Flowering persists from June to August, and the season's growth dies back each year, and can be cut to soil level or to living wood each February. Its hybrids are much more handsome and highly coloured, and "Grace Darling" with hyacinth-like, rosy-carmine flowers; "Countess of Onslow", bright violet-purple; and "Gravetye Beauty", rich deep red, are outstanding.

## GENERAL CULTURE UNDER GLASS

The needs of Clematis under glass are similar to their needs out of doors. Plants can be placed directly in the soil beds or borders. This permanent planting suits the more tender species and varieties in particular. The soil should be well drained, and this implies an initial deep trenching and some enrichment of the sub-soil with limestone grit or chalk crumbs if at all sticky. The soil itself should be loamy, with rotted organic matter, and coarse bone-meal at six to eight oz. per square yard, will be of benefit for several years. Finally, the top-soil will need lime to bring the pH to the near neutral (pH 7·0) level. With an annual top mulching with good rotted manure or compost, the plants thrive for many years. The root run can be kept cool by careful choice of the planting site, out of the direct hot rays of summer sun, and it is useful to grow a low top covering of plants such as ferns, or primulas.

An alternative way is to grow the plants in pots or containers such as red cedar, teak or rot-resistant wood boxes. The pots can be sunk to rim level in the soil so as to achieve even soil temperature and ease watering control. The pot naturally restricts root expansion, and to some extent, this is reflected in somewhat diminished top growth. This is not undesirable in the case of too rampant growers, or where the space available is limited. The plants suffer nothing in performance, provided the soil compost is well constituted, both physically and nutritionally.

A plant received from the nurseryman in its 4½-inch pot can be transferred into a 6-inch pot for its first year with the gardener, and then on into an 8½-, 9½- or 12-inch pot, according to its vigour, a year later (*see Chapter 9 for methods, timing, and soil compost formulae*). In subsequent years, an inch or two of the top soil will need to be removed and replaced with fresh compost, and when performance begins to fall off, with growth becoming weak and spindly and flower colour not so sparkling, repotting or replacement with a younger plant will have to be considered.

One of the advantages of growing the plants in pots is that the hardy kinds need not be under glass all the year round. They can be placed out of doors with their pots plunged in ashes to the rim as soon as flowering is over and they may be left like this throughout the winter, pruned according to their kind; they may be brought in again when they are in bud, for their flowering period. This sequence is useful where there is a conservatory or glassed-in passages to be furnished with summer blooms.

Under natural conditions, the roots of Clematis range widely and feed heavily, and when confined in pots, they repay generously for food during growth. At no time should they lack moisture during active growth from early spring to autumn, when they should be watered freely and generously with the rise of temperature. On warm and sunny days, the plants will revel in being syringed freely.

Feeding should take place about once every five to ten days, from the time shoots begin to elongate until the flower buds begin to open, and then cease. Further feeding will tend to hasten flowering and the setting of seeds. For feeding purposes, dilute liquid manure, made by steeping a sackful of rotted farmyard, stable or sheep manure, in a barrel of water, and diluting to straw colour, is drawn off. Alternatively a proprietary liquid fertiliser can be used, or the John Innes Liquid Feed (15 parts by weight ammonium sulphate, 2·75 parts potassium nitrate, 2·25 parts mono-ammonium phosphate: used at ½ oz. per gallon of soft tepid water, freshly dissolved).

## Forcing Clematis Bloom

When grown under glass, there is a spontaneous tendency for Clematis to bloom a little ahead of those grown outdoors, and for everyday enjoyment there is no real cause for forcing. A minimum winter temperature of about 40 to 45° F., is all that is needed for the more tender kinds, while hardy Clematis, normally grown out of doors the year round, are in no danger in the greenhouse without heat.

None of the Garden Clematis dealt with in this book should be subjected to hard forcing. This does not mean that they cannot be forced, for any observant gardener will see them exhibited in flower ahead of their normal season at the spring shows. It is chiefly the spring and early-summer flowering Clematis that repay, and respond to, gentle forcing.

*C. alpina* and its forms, *C. macropetala, C. armandii,* and the large-flowered hybrids can be flowered earlier than their normal time by giving them gentle heat. Forms of *C. alpina* or *C. patens,* for instance, will come into flower in mid-March, two to four weeks ahead of normal blooming, by growing them in temperatures no more than 45 to 55° F., from mid-January. Similarly, the large-flowering hybrids of *C. florida, C.* x *jackmanii* and *C. lanuginosa* can be brought into flower earlier with a night temperature that does not exceed 55° F.

Before any Clematis plant is subject to forcing, however, it is vital that it should be thoroughly well established and strongly rooted in good soil, and of a flowering age. Plants in pots should be at least in their third year and in no smaller than 6-inch pots. They are best brought on into bud under cool conditions before being introduced into the heated warm greenhouse or conservatory. Under artificially warmed conditions, particular attention is needed to watering, and this should be done with tepid soft water at the same temperature as the greenhouse.

## Clematis in the Home

An indoor window framed in garlands of Clematis flowers is an unusual and delighting sight, but exceptional since Clematis are not particularly good plants to grow indoors in the home all the time. Most plants are far too rampant, and they do not thrive under house conditions as we should like.

Nevertheless, there is no reason why young plants should not be used for indoor decoration for short periods. For this purpose, young plants, well rooted in 6-inch pots, with their shoots trained up a three or four foot tall tripod of canes or a cylinder of wire trellis, and in full bloom, can be brought indoors to grace a room for about a week, and then placed out of doors or in a cold greenhouse. To keep them indoors longer may vitiate their annual growth. In any case, flowering falls off.

There is a dwarf variety *nana* of *C. viticella* which grows only three feet tall, with the blue-purple, scented flowers typical of the species, which is useful for pot culture with a view to indoor decoration.

# II

# THE HERBACEOUS CLEMATIS

HERBACEOUS: *Not woody, or, if somewhat woody, dying back each year.*

(of plants). *Not forming a persistent woody stem; may be annual, biennial, or perennial.*

*Dying down to the ground annually.*
(of plant organs). *Soft, green, having the texture of leaves.*

VARIOUS BOTANICAL DEFINITIONS

At the mention of Clematis, most gardeners think only of the large-flowered hybrid climbers, and not unreasonably, since these are the types most often displayed at shows, and advertised and written about in the popular gardening journals. There is, however, another section of the genus, the herbaceous Clematis, into which it is well worth delving, for the plants are botanically interesting, and make no mean contribution to garden adornment and amenity.

The earliest herbaceous species to be introduced into Britain was *Clematis integrifolia* from Southern Europe in 1573. This somewhat old-fashioned perennial still finds favour with discerning plantsmen, and is well suited to the mixed flower border. It grows erectly with slender but stout stems, two to three feet high, furnished with simple, entire, ovate, and pointed leaves 2½ to 4 inches long and stalkless, or almost so. The solitary, nodding, urn-shaped flowers are borne at the ends of stems and from the axils of the uppermost leaves on stalks of about 1½ inches, and measure one to two inches long, with four fleshy or leathery sepals of a velvety greyish-blue, and deeper blue on the outside, from June to August. There are white, violet, and other blue-coloured forms. Each year the stems die back and can be removed with the annual border tidying-up. Plants can be raised readily from seed, or the roots may be divided in early spring.

*C. integrifolia* seems to have had much attraction for breeders in the nineteenth century, for it became the parent of some notable hybrids to which it transmitted its herbaceous habit quite strongly. One of the more widely acclaimed of these hybrids is *C.* x *eriostemon*. Its raising, from a parentage of *C. integrifolia* x *C. viticella*, is attributed to a Mr. Henderson, of Pineapple Nursery, St. John's Wood, London, in 1835, who called it *C. hendersoni*, or Henderson's Virgin's Bower. It is also synonymous with *C. bergeronii*, *C.* x *chandleri*, and *C.* x *intermedia*.

*C.* x *eriostemon* throws up slender stems to six to eight feet each year, which die back to the ground each winter. The leaves are entire, the lower ones simple and ovate, the upper pinnate, with ovate leaflets up to two inches long, while the flowers are solitary, bell-shaped, with four spreading sepals of a deep bluish purple, and a central tuft of greenish stamens, measuring two to three inches across. They are produced in much abundance from July to September, and although the flower-heads tend to bend sharply downwards, the plant is very attractive in flower, with a sweet, somewhat fugitive, scent. It can be grown effectively up tripods or posts to the rear of borders, or up walls, pillars or fences with ease and success. It increases readily from half-ripe cuttings of young shoots taken in summer and inserted in a sandy loam on a cold frame, or from root division in the autumn.

The antecedents of *C.* x *aromatica* are not crystal clear, but it is definitely a herbaceous hybrid, believed to have originated about 1845. Wm. Robinson, who did so much to popularise the Clematis, thought *C. viticella* to be a parent, but more recent authorities believe it to be of *C. integrifolia* x *C. flammula* parentage. It makes a good plant for the flower border, producing slender, herbaceous stems up to six feet tall, with five-leafleted leaves, each leaflet entire, oval, and one to 1½ inches long; and bears deep bluish-violet flowers, up to 1½ inches across, giving a sweet, faintly aromatic fragrance, in loose, terminal cymes, with great abundance from July until the autumn.

*C.* x *durandii* (*C. integrifolia* x *C.* x *jackmanii*) is a distinctive and easily grown hybrid originating at Lyons, France, about 1870, which bears the larger flowers of the Jackman hybrid. The stems are stout, often growing to ten feet long, with simple, entire, ovate leaves, three to six inches long, on short stalks, and lovely dark blue-violet flowers, usually with four sepals, measuring three to 4½ inches across, with a central tuft of yellow stamens, produced freely from the axils, from June to September. In var. *pallida*, the flowers are of a paler violet-rose. Both plants can be grown with success in the flower border, requiring only light support such as pea sticks, or they can be grown up fences, trellis or pillars with equal distinction. The plant is not truly herbaceous, but the year's growth should be shortened to within two to three feet of ground level each February.

One of the best herbaceous perennials for the hardy flower border is *C. recta* (syn. *C. erecta*), introduced from Southern and Eastern Europe as long ago as 1597. Each year, its tufted stems, with large, six-inch long pinnate leaves, having five to seven ovate, pointed, entire leaflets of shiny green, grow three to four feet tall, and bear an abundance of small, four-sepalled, white flowers in loose terminal and axillary panicles, dispensing a sweet fragrance in the June-July garden. It needs little or no support, becoming more splendid with the years. There are several varieties, the best being *flore pleno*, with double flowers; *grandiflora*, with slightly larger, pure white flowers, and more of them than the type; and *purpurea*, which has purple foliage and bronzy-purple stems. Once established, all these plants make foamy masses of white, fragrant bloom in high summer.

America contributes several species of herbaceous habit, either naturally or in culture. One of the prettier species is the frilled or Marsh Clematis (*C. crispa*) which grows in the southern states of North America, from Virginia to Florida and Texas. In this country, it is a little tender, and the crowns of plants usually need winter protection. The stems grow out to eight to ten feet, but are of slender, even frail, grace, and need light support. The foliage is tri-foliate, and pinnate with thin, smooth, broadly ovate leaflets, and the solitary flowers, on stalks up to three inches long, are bell-shaped and nodding, with sepals, one to two inches long, recurving at the tips, bluish or pinkish-purple with paler margins, appearing in June and with successional bloom well into August, spreading a sweet fragrance in the garden. Each year, the season's growth is cut to within a few inches of ground level. Plants may be raised from seeds or by division of the roots.

Although introduced in 1730, *C. viorna*, the Leather Flower, native to the eastern states of North America, from Pennsylvania to Alabama, is chiefly of curiosity or botanical interest. It is a slender climber, producing stems of eight to ten feet, with pinnate leaves, made up of five to seven tri-lobed or tri-foliate, thin leaflets, and rather curious solitary flowers, pitcher-shaped, with thick, fleshy or leathery sepals of a dull reddish-purple, nodding on stout stalks of two to three inches length, in July. The stems die back to the ground each winter, when they should be removed.

One of the most interesting American species is the Scarlet Clematis, *C. texensis* (syn. *C. coccinea*), a native of Texas, which produces semi-woody, climbing stems of about six feet, sometimes more, which, in Britain, die back to the ground each winter. Its leaves are pinnate, with four to eight broad-ovate, thickish, glaucous, blue-green leaflets, one to three inches long, from the axils of which pitcher-shaped, solitary, nodding flowers, about one inch long, formed of four thick scarlet to carmine sepals with their tips reflexed, appear on long slender stalks in June to August, and persist for some time. It is a distinctive plant to grow, with support, in a warm border or on a wall or fence, and easily managed, since the dead growth is removed each February. The species has, however, gained greater importance as a parent of several large-flowering hybrids, but in these, the stems are perennial and persist from year to year.

*C. douglasii* is a dwarf species collected by David Douglas and introduced in 1889 from the Rocky Mountain states of Montana, Wyoming, and Washington, U.S.A. It grows about

95

1½ to two feet high, with double pinnate leaves, and narrow, deflexing, linear leaflets, and bell-shaped solitary, terminal flowers nodding on long, woolly stalks, made up of 1½-inch long, pointed sepals, deep purple within, and lighter purple outside, in May–June. It can be grown from seeds, and propagated by root division in early spring. A variety *scottii* is said to have more finely divided, fern-like foliage, and flowers more urn-shaped, with sepals slightly contracted at the end.

Another dwarf with short herbaceous stems, reaching one to two feet tall, is *C. fremontii*, a native of Kansas, Missouri and Nebraska states, U.S.A., but it is of no great garden quality. The leaves are simple, leathery, almost entire, broadly ovate, conspicuously veined and stiff, growing stalkless straight from the stem to three or four inches long, and the flowers are small, drooping, hyacinth-like, with thick purple sepals, produced at the top of the stems in July–August. It can be grown from seed and be propagated by root division in early spring.

It is also doubtful that the Japanese herbaceous species, *C. stans*, introduced in 1860, merits much attention. It is a half- or sub-shrub, producing herbaceous stems of erect growth to four or five feet, with dark green, downy ternate leaves, ovate and sharply toothed, the middle leaflet being much the largest, and nodding, tubular, hyacinth-like, small, pale-blue flowers, in terminal and axillary clusters, close to the head of the plant, in September.

The Manchurian species, *C. fusca*, first seen in Britain in 1860, is again more of a collector's plant, although quite pretty. It produces vigorous growth in semi-herbaceous stems of eight feet or more, graced with pinnate leaves of five to seven, entire, ovate leaflets of 1½ to 2½ inches long, and small, solitary, urn-shaped, flowers, of four to five sepals, woolly and reddish-brown on the outside, violet within, on short, hairy stalks, in June. It may be readily grown from seeds, and needs cutting back to live wood each February.

Another sub-shrub, tending to become woody at the base, but producing herbaceous stems, stiffly erect to three feet, is *C. heracleifolia*, a native of North China and Mongolia, and at one time known as *C. mongolica* and *C. tubulosa*, and introduced into

*ematis armandii*. This is a very vigorous climber for a sheltered wall, growing to feet. Flowers are either white or pink in April-May.

*Clematis lasustern*. A deep blue which later fades to campanula blue. Flowers May-Jun
and August-September.

Britain in 1837. It is rather notable for its long-stalked, large, ternate, leaves of bright green and rather coarse, the middle leaflet being up to five inches long. The flowers are small and tubular, with blue sepals, and very much like those of a single hyacinth, and are produced freely in terminal and axillary corymbs in August and September, giving off a pleasant scent. The variety *davidiana*, however, introduced in 1864 by Abbé David, is a finer form, taller, with flowers of a somewhat deeper blue and with longer and more spreading sepals. "Côte d'Azur", with deep sky-blue flowers, and "Campanile", with flowers of a pale azure blue, are also good varieties, of erect and graceful habit, which make quite striking plants for the late summer flower border. All may be propagated by division in early spring, or by cuttings in summer.

The remaining herbaceous species are seldom offered today, and are not of very outstanding garden merit. *C. songarica* (syn. *C. gebleriana*), introduced in 1880 from Asian countries ranging from Siberia to Turkestan, is somewhat weed-like, throwing herbaceous stems to four or five feet, with simple, narrow, linear to lanceolate, bluish-green leaves, two to four inches long, and small, glossy, greenish yellow-white flowers freely produced in terminal and axillary clusters from July to September, and ripening to silky, plumose seed heads. It is a suitable plant for the semi-wild garden, or its stems may be trained up rough supports. The stems die back annually to a woody base, and should be removed in February.

The Chinese *C. ranunculoides*, introduced in 1906, has claimed little attention. Its herbaceous stems are purplish-red and grooved, growing to six feet, with tri-foliate foliage lower down, and pinnate higher up the plant, and small purple-rose, four-sepalled flowers, solitary or in small panicles from the leaf axils or the ends of shoots in summer. It seems best suited to the edges of woodland, or the wild garden.

## THE CULTURE OF HERBACEOUS CLEMATIS

This group of Clematis succeed in most soils which are reasonably well-drained, and provided with lime. They are somewhat gross feeders, and welcome an annual top-dressing of rotted farmyard manure or good compost. Their position in a flower border should usually be from mid-distance to the rear, where their roots may enjoy some shade from neighbouring plants, and where their flowering is seen to perfection.

Most of the herbaceous plants give a better display when their stems are given support. It is often suitable to let them clamber through a few tall pea-sticks or a slender tripod of canes, to a height at which their tips can arch over gracefully. Even the stiffish, erect-growing perennials, such as *C. recta*, *C. douglasii*, *C. integrifolia*, *C. heracleifolia* and its varieties are the better for some support.

Each year, the stems need to be cut back or removed to their base about February, before the new growth begins.

# 12

# CLEMATIS DISEASES AND PESTS

*Thus are my blossoms blasted in the bud,*
*And caterpillars eat my leaves away.*

WM. SHAKESPEARE
*Henry VI, Part 2, III, i, 89*

O NE OF the most estimable virtues of the Clematis genus is its immunity to all but a handful of diseases and pests. The well-established Clematis plant is unlikely to suffer injury under normal care, and there is no necessity for any routine spraying or dusting with fungicides or insecticides as may be the case with other flowers, such as Roses.

*Clematis Wilt.* This is one of the oldest and the most serious diseases afflicting Clematis plants. It has been known for over fifty years, and has been investigated and re-investigated during that time, but no full elucidation of the exact cause has yet been made.

The disease affects plants of two years old or more, as a rule. It strikes suddenly in early summer, when one or more of the shoots wilt and die-back as if cut through or girdled. The leaf blades and leaflets hang downwards and quickly wither and die. Sometimes the whole plant is involved, sometimes just one or more stems are affected.

Almost invariably, wilt comes with a shocking suddenness to plants apparently flourishing in perfect health a few days before. Usually, it is found that the place on the stems above which growth has died is at or about the soil level, sometimes a little above, sometimes slightly below; sometimes at a node, sometimes between nodes. It has been suggested that some injury to the bark by tools, weather, insect pest or animal, gives entry to the parasitic fungus, but signs of such damage are not invariably present.

In America, somewhat similar, but apparently more clearly defined, symptoms of wilt, have been attributed to a leaf-spotting fungus, *Ascochyta clematidina* (Thum.) Gloy, and the disease is known as Stem Rot. In a report (New York (Geneva) Agricultural Experimental Station Technical Bulletin, 44, 1–14, 1915), Mr. W. O. Gloyer gave *Ascochyta clematidina* as the cause of stem rot and leaf spot of Clematis.

The disease may be evident as a stem rot alone or as a leaf spot and a stem rot; the former usually occurring out of doors and attacking the stems near the soil, and the latter under glass. The leaves are affected by small water-soaked spots, which become buff-coloured with reddish margins, and the fungus may advance down the petioles into the stems, girdling them and killing the growth above, or independent internodal infections may occur, causing individual shoots to wilt suddenly and die. Pycnida (fruiting bodies) may be produced on either leaf or stem lesions, and infection or re-infection arise from spores shed by them.

The measures suggested to control stem rot in America are the collection and destruction of dead and diseased leaves and stems, and spraying or dusting with a fungicide, of which a sulphur fungicide is apparently the most successful.

It is not confirmed, however, that the disease we know in Britain as wilt and American stem rot and leaf spot are one and the same, as the fungus *Ascochyta clematidina* has yet to be identified in association with wilt. For the prevention and control of wilt, therefore, we have to fall back upon somewhat empirical methods.

It has been observed that plants grown on their own roots are less susceptible to wilt than those on grafted rootstocks, and also that when infected, they are more likely to throw up fresh shoots from the base and so recover. Wilt control, therefore, begins in the planting of Clematis plants growing on their own roots. Fortunately, the best of firms specialising in Clematis now send out plants on their own roots. If grafted stock is knowingly planted, it is wise to set the plants with the graft union below soil level, so that the variety may be encouraged to make its own roots.

If wilt does strike, treatment will depend on its severity. Should the whole plant collapse, it is sensible to remove it completely and burn, rather than leave it as a centre from which new infection may spread. When only some stems wilt, these stems should be cut out completely to their base, or to just above a node of healthy wood below the point of girdling, and the cut surface painted with a fungus-resistant paint (Medo, a paste of powdered sulphur and soft soap, white lead paint, or Stockholm Tar). Any fallen leaves should be gathered and burnt.

*Mildew.* The whitish-grey, dust-like covering of plant leaves known as powdery mildew may affect Clematis plants under unfavourable conditions. The trouble is rarely serious or severe, and does not appear until the late summer, as a rule. Plants growing in very hot positions, draughty situations, and under conditions where changes of humidity and temperature are apt to be severe, are most likely to suffer. The fungi responsible, *Erysiphe communis* and *E. polygoni*, are common as they often infect other plants, but they are superficial and easily controlled if prompt action is taken. Spraying or dusting with Karathane or a fungicide based on Thiram or sulphur gives an immediate check to the fungi.

Isolated damage may sometimes be done to foliage or flowers by leaf-spotting fungi and rust occasionally appears on leaves and stems, but can usually be adequately controlled by the removal and destruction of affected parts.

*Insect Pests.* Few insects take much toll of Clematis plants. Leaf-eating caterpillars, normally associated with fruit trees, such as those of the winter moth (*Operophtera brumata*), the mottled umber moth (*Hybernia defoliaria*), and tortrix moths (*Cacoecia podana, C. crataegana, Tortrix diversana*), may feed on and destroy the growing tips and leaves of young tender shoots in spring. They can be easily controlled, however, by a single spraying of the plants with a malathion, gamma-BHC or DDT insecticide when damage is noted.

Brown soft scale (*Lecanium coryli*) may sometimes appear on the bark, and the smoky-brown shells, about ¼ inch long, may be mistaken for wart-like excrescences or fungous growths, but are the remains of the dead female, under which lie maturing offspring. A spring spraying with a malathion, gamma-BHC or DDT insecticide, about April, will effectively check infestation.

Below ground, the grubs of cockchafer or may bug (*Melolontha melolontha*) and the garden chafer (*Phyllopertha hirticola*) may feed on the roots of Clematis, but need to be present in force to do noticeable harm. Wireworms, the larvae of click beetles, may also do some damage to root systems. Full protection can be given against such soil pests, however, by dressing the soil with an aldrin soil insectidal dust when planting in ground suspected of infestation. This is a wise precaution to take when planting in ground recently converted from pasture, lawn or grassland.

Infestation of Clematis by eelworms or nematodes has received scant attention, and is apparently not very common. Nevertheless, where it has been observed, it has been found that the root-knot eelworm, *Heterodera marioni*, is responsible. This organism is cosmopolitan, and has a wide range of plant hosts, including tomatoes, lettuce, and many weeds. When a Clematis plant shows signs of backward, stunted growth, and a tendency to unhealthy colour or yellowing in foliage, not attributable to any other discernible source, the roots should be bared and examined. Infestation reveals itself in galls or swellings on the roots of varying size, distorting the roots if numerous. The trouble often appears on plants grown in borders under glass. It is usually necessary to lift the plants, cut away the infested roots and burn them, and sterilize the soil by steam treatment before replanting. Alternatively, the soil can be watered with a dilute solution of parathion (1 part to 66 parts water, applied with care, using 1 gallon per square yard.) As parathion is a scheduled poisonous substance under the Agricultural (Poisonous Substances) Regulations of 1952 and 1955, it must be handled and applied only when wearing rubber boots, rubber gloves, overall, hood and face-shield. The treated soil should be left at least fourteen days before being handled.

*Slugs and Snails.* There is something in Clematis tissue, possibly its sweet alkaline calcium content, highly attractive to slugs and snails, particularly the former, which make these molluscs highly destructive. They are especially harmful in the milder spells of weather from the beginning of the year to early summer.

Slugs are the most destructive because they usually operate in greater numbers. The grey slug, *Agriolimax reticulatus*, and the large black slug, *Arion ater*, and black field Slug, *Arion hortensis*, do much damage by eating young, tender, developing shoots at and above soil level, while the keeled or subterranean slugs, *Milax gagates* and *M. sowerbii*, work below the surface of the soil as well. Snails have similar habits, and while the garden snail, *Helix aspersa*, is the more noticeable, small snails, such as *Helix rufescens*, may often be found quite high up on plants devouring foliage.

These pests are nocturnal in habit, and are quite capable of reducing Clematis plants to death within a few nights if unchecked. Apart from damage to young stems and foliage, they often rasp away at the bark and girdle stems for several inches from the ground. Clematis on walls or fences are apt to suffer severely, since these supports give hiding places where the pests can lay up during the day.

Fortunately, there are several effective ways of controlling slugs and snails. Newly planted Clematis can be protected by a nine to twelve inch sleeve of polythene, a tall empty tin can with both ends cut out, or a collar of tinplate, galvanised sheet iron or zinc, around the crown of the plant, with weathered coal or coke ashes about the protective collar.

The crown of established plants can also be protected from occasional forages of slugs in winter by covering them with coal or coke ashes until early spring.

The most effective chemical control is metaldehyde, which

can be used in a number of ways. A bait can be prepared, using 1 oz. crushed or powdered metaldehyde to 3 lb. bran, dried tea leaves, or bone-meal, and scattering this lightly over the soil around the crowns of plants on mild, damp evenings in spring or summer. It remains effective longer if protected from the weather, and small heaps placed eight to twelve inches apart, under tiles, flat stones, slates, wooden boards, or halves of orange or grapefruit, attract the slugs, and remain unaffected by rain or eaten by birds. There are also proprietary ready-made metaldehyde baits in pellets on the market, which are weather-resistant.

Plant stems and foliage can be protected by spraying them with a suspension solution of metaldehyde* or with a solution of powdered alum (1 oz. per two gallons water), which lasts for seven to ten days or until rain washes it off. Another measure is to ring plants with a dusting of a mixture of equal parts by weight of powdered copper sulphate and ground limestone, and to dust the mixture at the base of pillars, walls or fences where the molluscs find shelter. The copper sulphate is toxic, and the limestone is added to neutralise the acidifying effect of copper sulphate on the soil. One pound of the mixture is ample for about twenty square yards of ground.

It is always instructive to go out at dusk, hunting the slugs and snails, on a mild night of spring or summer, with a torch. The numbers that can be collected are often astonishing, even on consecutive nights. The pests can be disposed of by dropping them into a bucket of water to which a little salt, copper sulphate or alum has been added. Complete eradication in highly infested areas seems impossible, for slugs and snails will invade favoured conditions from elsewhere. Across paths, their slime trails often betray them, and dusting such paths with powdered copper sulphate will deter them. Reducing organic rubbish and maintaining a good hygienic standard of cleanliness and tidiness in the garden generally, gives fewer refuges to the mollusc parasites.

*Mice and Bank Voles* may do damage to Clematis by eating

* Slugit.

buds, growing points and young leaves in winter and early spring. It is possible to reduce their numbers by trapping with break-back traps, or baiting with warfarin, but extermination is more difficult. Where the main colonies can be located, it is useful to stop all but a few strategically chosen holes. Put Toplin fuses down these holes, and cover the area with a polythene sheet, after lighting the fuses, so the fumes may be enclosed.

In gardens where rabbits are troublesome, the simplest way of protecting Clematis is to use a repellent (Renardine and Animoil are proprietary brands). A length of soft twine, soaked in the solution, and strung on short sticks, four to six inches high, around the crown of the plant to be protected, is sufficient, until the rabbits can be eradicated.

*Kinking.* This is not a disease but a mechanical injury which is often disastrous to young plants. It can occur when planting, for young Clematis stems are rather brittle, and it can be caused by careless use of the hoe or tools about the plant resulting in the stem being caught and suddenly bent or kinked. The bark is fractured, and this, in itself, is enough to disrupt growth and cause die-back, though it also may admit parasitic fungi.

Clematis plants cannot be planted too carefully. If the plant is already trained and fastened to a cane, it is wise to leave the cane in position, at all events until the plant is established and making new growth. Plants coming from the nursery bed are best given a cane and fastened to it before moving. Good nurseries send out plants in pots, ready staked, and others should be regarded with suspicion. In cultivation, it is better to weed about the crowns with the hands and avoid accidents with tools. Much disturbance of the soil over the roots is unnecessary if the plants receive annual top-dressings of rotted organic material.

# *13*

# PROPAGATING CLEMATIS

*In the morning sow thy seed, and in the evening*
*withhold not thine hand; for thou knowest not*
*whether shall prosper, either this or that, or*
*whether they both shall be alike good.*

ECCLESIASTES, I I, 6

I T IS the privilege of the gardener to be instrumental in the creation of new plants, and the glowing thrill at the first appearance of a seedling of his own sowing above ground, or the elongation of the buds of a cutting of his own preparation into new shoots, is wonderfully rewarding and rich with a deep feeling of accomplishment. Happily, in the Clematis genus, the gardener will find ample scope for the exercise of his interest and his skill in propagation. New Clematis plants can be raised from seeds, cuttings, layers, or increased by grafting and division.

## CLEMATIS FROM SEEDS

The majority of the species and their varieties can be successfully raised from seeds. Most of them set and ripen their seeds freely in Britain, though this is not often the case in very late flowering kinds like *C. paniculata*. The temptation to use the seeds from one's own plants is strong, and there is no reason why we should not give way to it, provided the seeds are well ripened. It must also be kept in mind that there will be some variation in the resultant seedlings, and not all of them will reflect parental characteristics faithfully. They will vary in vigour as well as flower and foliage character, and it is necessary to select the best for retention, as soon as the behaviour of the seedlings can be properly discerned.

In a garden containing a collection of Clematis, some variation in the seedling plants may arise from cross-pollination carried out by natural agencies such as bees. While it is fascinating to raise seedlings that carry the promise of hybrid qualities, it is likely to be more rewarding and more successful if planned along the lines of selective hybridisation than if left to chance.

Home-saved seeds are best taken from flowers selected for their perfect character—not the earliest nor the latest to open, but those borne during the flush of strong growth when the plant is moving to its climax of bloom. Seeds of many species and varieties can be bought from seedsmen specialising in them.

The seeds of Clematis are contained in one-seeded achenes or small, dry, hard, indehiscent (not opening to release the seed) fruits, usually—but not always—with long, persistent styles, feathered with silky hairs. Such enclosed seeds are slow to germinate, as moisture and air must seep through achene and seed coats before life is quickened in the seed.

Seeds of the early-flowering species and varieties such as *C. alpina* and *C. montana* are usually ripe enough to sow in late summer and early autumn, and may be expected to germinate in the late winter or early spring of the following year.

The seeds are best sown in seed pans or boxes suitably prepared. Good drainage is essential, and the pans should be crocked, and the crocks covered with a thin layer of beech leaves or sphagnum moss to prevent soil working down and blocking drainage. A well-drained soil compost is needed. A mixture of equal parts by bulk medium loam, rotted leaf-mould and coarse sand, plus 1 oz. bone flour and $\frac{3}{4}$ oz. ground chalk or limestone per bushel answers quite well. Or the John Innes formula of two parts by bulk medium sterilised loam, two parts horticultural sedge or moss peat and one part coarse sand, plus $1\frac{1}{2}$ oz. superphosphate and $\frac{3}{4}$ oz. ground chalk or limestone per bushel, can be used to give unvarying results.

Although good drainage is important, it is just as vital that the soil should not dry out. To this end, especially when seeds are slow in germination, it is very helpful to add up to one third of horticultural vermiculite (grade 5) to the compost, whichever formula is used. This material assures good aeration together with moisture retention, and seedlings can be lifted from the pans for potting on with more roots intact.

The pans need soaking by immersion and then draining off before sowing. Seed may be sown at $\frac{1}{8}$ to $\frac{1}{4}$ inch deep. They should be covered with a sifting of sand or fine grade vermiculite, and this should be firmed by a light watering from a fine-rose can or syringe. The pans (or boxes) are then covered with a slate or tiles—the brown paper and glass method is less suitable for slow-germinating seeds—and placed in a cool or cold frame, which is then closed. From time to time, the pans should be examined, and if necessary, watered to prevent drying out. The frame remains closed otherwise until germination takes place.

If no frame is available, the seed-pans can be placed sunk to their rims in ashes or soil in the shelter of a north wall, though germination may not take place until April or May.

When the first wiry shoots of germinating seedlings break through the soil, they should gradually and progressively be given more light and air. The covers are removed. The frames are opened for ventilation in the warmer mid-hours of the day, and as the seedlings grow, they can be placed nearer the glass. They should not be exposed to very strong or hot sunlight, however.

As soon as the seedlings are large enough to handle, they should be carefully removed with as little damage to the roots are possible, and potted into $2\frac{1}{2}$-inch (thumb) or 3-inch (60's) pots, singly; the soil compost can be one of three parts by bulk sifted medium loam, one of leaf-mould (or peat), one of coarse sand, plus 3 oz. bone flour and 1 oz. ground chalk or limestone per bushel. Or better still, the John Innes Potting Compost of seven parts by bulk sterilised medium loam, three parts horticultural moss or sedge peat, two parts coarse sand, plus $\frac{3}{4}$ oz. ground chalk or limestone, $1\frac{1}{2}$ oz. hoof and horn meal, 1½ oz. superphosphate and ¾ oz. sulphate of potash per bushel, will answer splendidly.

The seedlings should be potted quite firmly but carefully, watered, and returned to the frame to be kept close for a few days until over the shock of transplanting, and then given increasing ventilation, as the weather and growth warrant. Such young plants can be potted on into 4½-inch (48's) or 6-inch (32's) pots in the following autumn or spring. As seeds germinate irregularly, the seed pans should not be emptied until sufficient seedlings have been obtained. It takes about two years to grow a flowering plant from seed, which can be planted out in permanent quarters.

In the case of the late-flowering Clematis, and these include the large-flowered hybrids, the seed should be sown in March. Exactly the same procedure is followed as that outlined for the autumn-sown, early-flowering kinds, but the seed pans often have to remain in the closed frame until the following spring before germination occurs. Sometimes, germination is delayed to fifteen or eighteen months, and correspondingly, the plants only flower two and a half to three years after sowing.

The herbaceous species such as *Clematis recta*, *C. heracleifolia* and *C. integrifolia* are raised from seeds sown under glass in March in the greenhouse or frame, and germinate more readily, giving plants that are usually ready for planting out in summer or autumn.

The greenhouse species, *C. indivisa* and its var. *lobata*, are best raised from seeds sown in February in a warm greenhouse, with initial temperature of 65° to 70° F. The same techniques and composts are used, except that the plants are grown on under glass entirely.

Many Clematis species and varieties, and some of the hybrids, will also germinate more readily, within a month or two of sowing, when sown in a warm greenhouse, with a bottom-heat of 65° to 70° F., in February; and the seedlings can later be potted on and transferred to cold frames for the summer, often giving flowering plants within eighteen months.

In all instances, the more reliable and speedier germination is likely to come from well-ripened, fresh seeds.

### CLEMATIS FROM CUTTINGS

Most of the Clematis can be most readily increased by means of vegetative propagation, whereby a part of a plant is taken and induced to root and form a separate plant on its own. The method is particularly important in the case of plants of hybrid origin, which do not reproduce themselves perfectly from seeds. Of the various methods of vegetative propagation, the taking and rooting of cuttings give us new plants, true to type, most quickly.

In the case of Clematis, the simplest technique is to take cuttings of half-ripe or maturing shoots of the current year's growth during the summer months. The shoots should be of robust, healthy growth, and may be two to four inches long, according to the type of plant.

The cut may be made about ½ inch below a node, or halfway between two nodes on the stem. Much has been said and written about the taking of internodal cuttings of Clematis but the advantage is chiefly one of convenience. It is held that the rooting power is largely determined by the presence of a growth-regulating substance, produced at or near the buds of

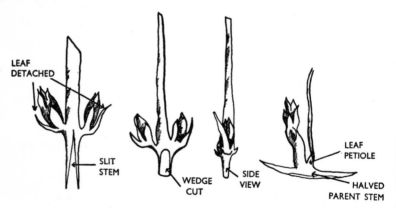

1. Internodal cutting     2. Nodal cutting          3. Cutting of a
                                                    lateral bud through
                                                    the node

*CUTTINGS OF CLEMATIS*

nodes and most concentrated a little below the nodes, and which is sent down the stem.

Clematis cuttings root just as readily from the node as from between nodes. Where the nodes are conveniently near together, there is no special advantage in preparing internodal cuttings. A cut can be made just below a node at the base, and just above the node from which growth is desired at the top of the cuttings. When there are several inches between nodes, as in several large-flowering Clematis, it is more convenient to take an internodal cutting, with a basal cut made mid-way between two nodes.

In the case of some Clematis which make short, lateral shoots, such shoots can be taken with a "heel" of older wood, in late summer. *C. montana* is a species that can be propagated from such cuttings.

It is difficult to lay down exact dates for taking half-ripe cuttings, sometimes called soft-wood or green-wood cuttings, as the true guide is the living state of the shoot. It is best to avoid the soft leading points of the stems and shoots of great vigour. In hot, sunny summers, wood ripens more quickly and sooner than in cool, dull and wet summers. A reasonably fair guide is the tendency of the shoot to crack rather than just bend and recover, when sharply bent.

Broadly, cuttings of most of the smaller-flowering Clematis, such as *C. afoliata*, *C. alpina*, *C. calycina*, *C. chrysocoma*, *C. flammula*, *C. macropetala*, and their varieties, can usually be taken from late July to September. Several of the large-flowering kinds, such as those of the Florida, Lanuginosa, Patens and Texensis groups, will propagate from cuttings taken at this time.

Half-ripe cuttings must have good aeration and moisture, plus warmth. The cuts should be clean, made with a sharp knife or razor blade, and it is helpful to slit them from the base up to half-way through the node, as this promotes root formation from both sides. The cuttings must be inserted in a well-drained rooting medium, and well firmed. Experts use clean, moist sharp sand, but this has little nutriment in it, and it requires a little judgment and skill to decide when rooting is sufficient to warrant a move to richer soil. The amateur will find it simpler to use horticultural vermiculite, which lessens watering worries, or the John Innes Cutting Compost of one part medium loam, two parts horticultural peat and three parts coarse, sharp or silver sand.

The cuttings are inserted with the top node just buried in the soil and the buds peeping out at the surface. Any leaves should, of course, be detached in preparing the cutting. Careful watering will firm the rooting medium well to the cutting.

Cuttings taken with a heel are inserted for about two-thirds their length in the rooting medium.

The cuttings can be inserted in pots or boxes, or in the soil of frames, and should be kept close in the frame until rooting. When cuttings are rooting and beginning to grow, they can be potted singly in 3- or 4½-inch pots, in a richer compost of John Innes Potting Compost No. 1, returned to the frame and kept close until growth begins to go forward again. Then they need ventilation and periodical watering.

The cuttings frame should be in a warm position, but shaded from direct hot sun. It is useful to maintain the necessary humidity by mist-spraying the cuttings daily in the morning, though excessive moisture is not desired.

Some of the hardy species will strike from cuttings inserted in a sandy soil in a warm, sheltered border, out of doors, covered with a bell-glass, jam jar, or open-ended box with a pane-of-glass lid. But for serious work, the use of a propagating frame is necessary.

On the other hand, several of the large-flowered hybrids will root best from nodal or internodal cuttings taken in late spring or early summer (May–June), and inserted in a greenhouse propagating frame, with bottom heat and a temperature maintained at 60° to 65° F. Such cuttings are of greener and softer shoots, and humidity by mist-spraying when there is the least chance of dryness should be maintained.

The new technique of propagating green or softwood cuttings by means of controlled mist spraying, together with heat and light, will no doubt make it possible to take many cuttings of Clematis early in the year, and advance the resultant plants to earlier flowering. At present, the cost of the equipment,

Clematis W. E. Gladstone. Slow climber to 10 feet
with large flowers, sometimes up to 9″. Lavender
flowers with purple anthers in July-October.

Mixed Clematis adds variety and an intermingled
display can often be flowering from April-October.

*Clematis macropetala.* Fast growing to 15 feet. Flowers April-May and a little in autumn.

*Clematis alpina.* Flowers April-May.

however, makes this method more a commercial proposition than one for the amateur.

Clematis cuttings can often be rooted with greater certainty by the use of one of the synthetic root-inducing growth-regulating (hormone) substances.* Care should be taken to choose the right strength for half-ripe cuttings. The prepared cutting is dipped in the material, usually a powder, prior to planting, and the cutting should be inserted with as little disturbance of the adhering powder as possible. The action of rooting is thereby speeded up, though the subsequent growth proceeds quite normally.

Some of the Clematis of herbaceous habit, such as *C.* x *durandii, C. heracleifolia* and its vars., and *C.* x *jouiniana,* may be propagated from cuttings taken in May, without much difficulty.

Often, plants from cuttings will produce good stems and start flowering within the following one or two years.

## CLEMATIS FROM LAYERS

The propagation of new Clematis plants from layers is the most foolproof, simple and satisfying method to use in the outdoor garden, and when only a limited number of plants are required. Layering gives plants on their own roots, which flourish excellently, reproducing all the quality of the parent plant. It can be practised with most of the species, varieties and hybrids.

The method of making a layer is simple. Selected, healthy and robust young shoots are earmarked, preferably at pruning time, for layering. They are shortened to five or seven feet, and bent to the ground. The layer is prepared by making a slanting cut of $1\frac{1}{2}$ to two inches, starting just behind a chosen node on the underside of the stem, and cutting upwards to bisect the node; or a notch can be cut immediately behind the node on the underside of the stem.

The prepared node is then pressed into the soil contained in a five- or six-inch pot, sunk to the rim in the ground at the

* Seradix B, made by May & Baker Ltd., Dagenham.

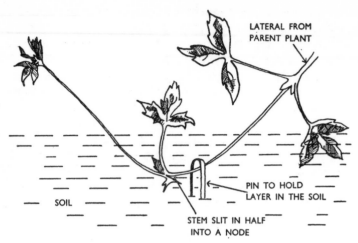

A layered shoot of *Clematis montana*

place where the layer can be bent to it without strain, and held in place by means of a layering pin (a piece of wire bent like a hairpin) or a small crotched wooden peg; the whole being covered with a well-firmed mound of soil, and a layer of moist peat or leaf-mould to give moist, cool rooting conditions. The soil in the pot should be either a well-drained sandy loam or the John Innes Cuttings Compost.

The cut surfaces of the prepared layer can be dusted with a root-inducing, growth-regulating "hormone" powder, though there is no difficulty in inducing roots to form from properly layered plants.

Although it is possible to layer the plants throughout the summer months while they are in active growth, it is best to do the work early in the year, before growth is too active, from about mid-February to early April. Early layering gives more strongly rooted and better plants, especially where the large-flowering hybrids are concerned. As a rule, the rooted layers are ready for severance from the parent plant by October or November. The more-slow-to-root kinds can be left until the following spring. Before severing and moving, the new growth should be shortened to eighteen to twenty-four inches and staked, so as to avoid mishap or damage to the somewhat brittle wood. The plants can be set out in their permanent positions in the normal way, and will flower the following year in most cases.

It is not always convenient or practical to layer shoots to the ground. In such instances, the modern technique of air-layering can be used. A suitable node is chosen and prepared by cuttings as for soil-layering. The cut surfaces are then treated with a root-inducing, growth-regulating substance of the appropriate strength in powder form.* A large handful of damp, clean sphagnum moss, which has been soaked in clear rainwater, is then needed. A few strands of the moss are carefully placed between the cut surfaces to keep the wound open, and the remainder of the moss wrapped and firmed around the node in a ball. This ball is then enclosed in a cylinder of sheet polythene film, preferably of ·004 or ·005 inches thickness.

The polythene film can be bought in a lay-flat tubular form, and a length of about seven inches of 6-inch width is suitable, or a piece of polythene about seven inches long and eight to ten inches wide, which can be wrapped around the moss, can be used. The overlap can be sealed by pressing the sides together with a hot iron before slipping it over the shoots as a cylinder; or it can be sealed with plastic tape (such as Sellotape) on the plant.

The bottom of the cylinder and the top are closed by sealing around the stem with insulating tape or plastic tape, so that no rain can seep in or moisture evaporate from the moss. In the moss sponge, air and moisture conditions are well-balanced and healthy, and the formation of roots is stimulated by the rooting compound. As the film is transparent, the rooting process can be watched, and as soon as the roots are seen to be filling the moss and growing to the outside of the ball, the layer is ready for severance.

Some care is needed. The film and tape are removed, and any moss that can be taken away without injuring the roots. The plant should then be potted into a 6-inch pot, with John Innes Potting Compost, placed in a cold frame, and kept close

* Seradix L.15, made by May and Baker Ltd., Dagenham.

and shaded until growth is actively resumed, when ventilation and light should be gradually increased. This type of air-layering can be attempted at any time during the growing season, but as with soil-layering, it is most successful when done in the early part of the year.

## CLEMATIS BY DIVISION

Propagation by dividing the roots of parent plants is chiefly practical with the herbaceous kinds of Clematis—*C. crispa, C. douglasii, C.* x *durandii, C.* x *eriostemon, C. fusca, C. heracleifolia, C. integrifolia, C.* x *jouiniana* and *C. stans.*

The plant to be divided is lifted carefully from the ground with roots intact before active growth begins, usually in late winter or early spring. The stock can then be divided with a sharp knife, removing suitable portions furnished with potential growing crown buds and with roots attached. In many cases, the divisions can be replanted at once in well-drained soil where they are to grow, being firmed, watered in, mulched with a little thoroughly rotted manure, and covered with a bell glass or cloche. Where the root portions yielded are small and vulnerable, it is best to pot them up in a well-drained compost (John Innes Cuttings Compost will suit), and place in a cold frame, kept close, until new roots are formed and new growth is evident. They can be given more air and light progressively, and after hardening off, be planted out where they are to grow. The parent plant can be replanted and will benefit from a liberal dusting of the soil with bone flour, and a top mulch of rotted manure.

One species, *C. glauca,* has the habit of forming suckers from the roots. These can be detached in autumn or in spring and planted out to give increase when required.

## THE GRAFTING OF CLEMATIS

By grafting we can unite two different but compatible plants of the same genus or family to grow as one plant. The technique is much used in plant propagation as a means of increasing desirable plants, particularly hybrids, quickly. The usual method is to graft the portion or scion of the desired plant on to the stem or roots—the stock—of an easily propagated and vigorous-rooting commoner species or variety.

This cannot be done without taking into account the mutual effect that scion and stock will have on one another. Usually, the vigour of the stock is allied to the desirable horticultural qualities of the scion to produce a strong plant. This works splendidly in the case of propagating hybrid roses, and with some reservations, in that of many tree fruits. In the case of Clematis, however, grafting has not proved an unqualified success.

Experience has proved that Clematis plants grown on their own roots are healthier, longer-lived and more satisfactory than those on a grafted root-stock, and far less subject to wilt or die-back disease. Nevertheless, grafting is a useful technique when it is desired to rush plants into growth and flowering so that their performance may be assessed. It is a somewhat tricky operation, however, for the inexperienced.

Clematis varieties are largely root-grafted on the root-stocks of *C. vitalba*, the wild native Traveller's Joy of Britain, or *C. viticella*, of southern Europe. As a rule, the chosen root-stocks are started into growth in late winter with heat in the greenhouse, and the scion-yielding plants a little later so that the scions are less advanced in their growth than the stocks. The stock is prepared by removing the top growth entirely, and the pieces of root to receive the scion are prepared for cleft-grafting by cutting a V-shaped notch in them. The scion is taken consisting of a single node from fairly soft new growth, cut and carefully fitted into the cloven stock, and with a matching of cambium layers. It is then bound with raffia and waxed, and the grafted plant is potted in a porous soil compost (John Innes Potting Compost) with the graft union below the surface, and placed in a warm frame, where moisture, air and temperature can be controlled. By spring, the plants are ready for hardening off and planting out.

The young growth is very vulnerable to injury, and susceptible to attack by pests or fungus parasites unless carefully husbanded and watched, and every principle of good culture should be observed to help the plant away to sound growth and the making of ripe wood. It is always sensible to plant out a graft with the union below soil level, and even mound soil to the stem of the scion with the intention of encouraging it to form its own roots in due course.

The amateur gardener buying in plants should insist on their being on their own roots, however. Fortunately, the better and more responsible of nurserymen specializing in the Clematis genus now offer their plants for sale on their own roots.

## $I\frac{4}{4}$

# HYBRIDISING THE CLEMATIS

*This is an art*
*Which does mend nature, change it rather, but*
*The art itself is nature.*

WM. SHAKESPEARE
*The Winter's Tale*, IV, 4

THE ART of hybridising and breeding plants has been
practised for thousands of years, but it is only since 1866, when
Gregor Mendel, an Austrian monk, published the results of his
investigations into the heredity of the garden pea, that some
understanding of the principles of Genetics has been gained.
Most of our scientific knowledge of heredity has been gained
within the present century, for it was only in 1900 that the
work of Mendel and the laws of heredity he had enunciated
became known and recognised by the world of botany at large.
Plant breeding, despite its ever-increasing formulation as a
science, still remains an art, and an art which every keen lover
of plants and their improvement can practise.

A hybrid plant is a plant raised by cross-fertilising two
different species, but the term is now often used to embrace
the progeny of any two plants yielding offspring. A hybrid
plant embodies inherited characteristics from both its parents,
some dominant and evident, others recessive and hidden. The
aim of hybridisation is to produce plants with those characteristics deemed desirable dominant in their growth and performance.

In practice, hybrid plants are produced by transferring the
pollen cells (or male gametes) from the flower of one selected

species or variety to the stigma of another so that they may join up with the ovules (or female gametes), and so form the fertile seeds from which the hybrid plants grow.

The flowers of the hardy Clematis are normally bisexual or hermaphrodite, with the male reproductive organs (the stamens) and the female (the pistil) being contained within them. An exception which might be noted is *C. heracleifolia* var. *davidiana*, which is dioecious, bearing only male flowers with stamens on one plant and female flowers with pistils on another.

The cross-pollination of any Clematis species or varieties can be attempted provided the stigma of the female flower at the end of the pistil is in a receptive, viscid condition at the time it is pollinated.

For straightforward working, it is desirable that the chosen plants should be blooming at the same time, and the flowers should be in the right state of readiness.

The minute pollen grains are formed within the small vessels known as anthers, situated at the tops of the stamens. When ripe, the minute powdery pollen is released and may be carried by air currents, insects or some natural agency to the stigma of the pistil. In its ripe condition, the stigma is shiny with a sticky sugary fluid, and pollen grains falling on it adhere. The sticky fluid is also essential to the further development of the pollen grains, which proceed to germinate and put forth a delicate pollen tube. Each pollen tube grows down the tissue of the style to the ovary, carrying with it the male cell or gamete, and when a pollen tube reaches an ovule, the male gamete can unite with the female, and fertilisation takes place. The fertilised ovule then develops into a seed, carrying the hereditary material of its parent plants.

When we desire to create new hybrid plants by cross-fertilisation we have to circumvent the natural, leave-it-to-chance methods of nature. In the case of the Clematis, after having determined the two species to be hybridised, it is necessary to emasculate the flower of the female or seed parent plant by removing all its anthers before any pollen is released. This must be done, as a rule, when the flower is still in the advanced bud or just opening stage. The sepals and the petals should be carefully cut away with fine-pointed, sharp scissors, and the anthers removed by severing their stamens with fine forceps or scissors.

If any pollen has been shed and has fallen on the stigma—a point easily checked by examination with a pocket lens or magnifying glass—the flowers should not be used.

After emasculation, the chosen seed flowers should be enclosed in a small loose polythene or fine muslin bag, to keep stray unwanted pollen out, until the stigma is in a viscid receptive state. Then, preferably on a fine bright day, the pollen of the chosen male parent can be placed on the stigma. There are several ways of doing this. Pollen can be gathered from the anthers with a camel-hair brush and transferred to the stigmas; or it can be done by removing stamens with fine forceps and shaking their anthers over the stigmas, or by shaking the male flower itself over the female so that its pollen falls on the stigmas.

Pollination is successful when a fair amount of pollen remains on the stigma. If it does not, then pollination should be repeated after two or three days. Immediately after pollinating a seed flower, the covering bag should be replaced. For the best results, it is not only necessary to choose first-class representative flowers as parents, but to carry out pollination as soon as the condition of the stigma and the pollen permit.

When the stigma and styles wither, the covering bags may be taken off, and the seed will ripen in about twelve to sixteen weeks from the time of pollination. The seeds are mature and ripe for gathering when they separate readily from the spent flower heads, and may then be sown as already discussed in the previous chapter.

Under average garden conditions, straight-forward hybridisation gives a high percentage of successful fertilisations. The first cross between two different species will give hybrid plants with characteristics of both parents, and from these plants the gardener can select any with outstanding qualities for further propagation by vegetative means.

It is most easy to cross species or varieties which flower at about the same time, since fresh pollen can be used at the time when it is most potent. If we wish to cross-pollinate plants of somewhat dissimilar flowering periods, then we must either advance or retard the flowering of one of the parents by growing it under artificially controlled conditions under glass, or when the male parent flowers ahead of the female, collect and store pollen for later use.

Ripe Clematis pollen can usually be kept for a few weeks if it is kept perfectly dry. The anthers should be carefully taken from the flowers when just about to burst, and placed in an envelope or screw of tissue paper, which in turn is placed in a corked test-tube or phial, which can be made airtight, together with a little silical gel to absorb moisture. The pollen can then be used when the seed parent flower is ready.

Most Clematis species cross-fertilise readily since their chromosome numbers are similar. Chromosomes are the small bodies, found in the nuclei of all cells, which carry the genes or units of inheritance that determine the inheritable characters of organisms. There are normally two similar sets of chromosomes present in all vegetative cells, known as the diploid number or $2n$. The sexual reproductive cells, however, normally contain half this number, called the haploid number or $n$. Nearly related species often have the same number of chromosomes. In Clematis, the diploid number or $2n=16$. An exception, however, is *Clematis paniculata*, which may have 16, 48, or 64.

It follows that in all crosses of compatible species or varieties, the gamete of each parent plant provides a haploid number of chromosomes which pair up in the fertilised egg or zygote of the resultant seed, and the plant resulting from such a seed inherits characteristics or genetical influences from both parents, and has a diploid number of chromosomes.

We can, of course, cross-fertilise more than one pair of flowers of the same parent plants, and obtain many seeds. If we grow all the seedling plants on until they flower, we shall find that some plants are better or finer in certain characteristics than others. There is a chance that a plant may arise with such beauty of flowering or habit that it is worth propagating for its distinction and this can be done by vegetative means of cuttings, layers and grafts. The majority of the hybrids and varieties now available in the Clematis have arisen in this way.

The chances of worthwhile variations arising from simple hybridisation can be increased by the use of different parents, or a cross can be made using the parent plants in reverse in their sexual roles. Whatever is done, however, careful notes and labelling of the crosses should be made as the work progresses.

Variations in the growth, development and character of plants are controlled and largely determined by the genes, and the role of the chromosomes is to provide a physical or mechanical basis for the transmitting and combining of genes. As the genes are exceedingly numerous, possibly numbering several thousands, the range of different combinations in breeding is enormous.

Beyond the prospect of raising some outstanding novelty from the hybrids (usually designated $F_1$ hybrids) of a simple first cross, lies the virtually unexplored ground of raising new Clematis from further cross-fertilisations of hybrid races, and back-crossing of hybrids with species. There is not space to go into this fascinating subject in this book, but it is in such hybridising adventure that such desirables as finer colour, wilt-resistance, and better habits of growth will be discovered. Compared with the hybridisation of the Rose, that of the Clematis is in its earliest stages.

## *15*

## CLEMATIS FLOWERS FOR INDOORS

*The hardy Clematis has been converted from an
ordinary climbing shrub to one of the most gorgeous of ornaments, unrivalled as a flowering
climber.*

THOMAS MOORE AND GEORGE JACKMAN
*The Clematis as a Garden Flower,* 1872

IN RECENT years, there has been a lively and growing
interest in the arrangement and use of cut flowers for the
indoor decoration of our homes, offices, shops and public
buildings. Yet in all the words that have been poured out on
this subject in books, lectures and demonstrations, there has
been but very meagre mention of the merits of Clematis flowers,
and comparatively little use of their graceful elegance, distinctive beauty, charming qualities has been made, except by the
discerning and knowledgeable few.

Too often it is thought that the Clematis flower, so magnificent in the garden, has no staying power when cut, and must
therefore fail when brought indoors. This, however, is not
strictly true, if the right type of plant material is chosen.
Flowers cut from the young, softish growths do falter and flag,
but if they are taken with a little older wood, cut slantingly,
or slit up a little, they can take up water more freely and
retain their turgidity to last and remain fresh for many days.

It is the nature of these climbing plants to produce their
flowers in sprays along the length of hanging shoots, and when
well grown, such shoots are lavishly furnished with bloom. They
lend themselves supremely well to arrangements of grace and

elegance in many ways, particularly for table decorations where they make beautiful runners; for the ornament of windows, the beautifying of pillars and posts, and look most charming when arranged in a vase or container on a pedestal from which they are draped in their natural habit. For the flower arranger of the modern school, Clematis open up a virtually unexplored resource, for the sprays of the smaller flowering species and varieties of the Viticella group have the simple purity of line so often desired, and many of the large-flowered hybrids make promising material.

Of the species, *C. campaniflora* provides sprays wreathed in dainty, nodding, white, tinged violet flowers; *C. flammula*, freely produced, fragrant, pure white flowers in panicles; *C. viticella*, small purple-blue, nodding, saucer flowers; and *C. orientalis*, with *C. tangutica*, gives yellow flowers during late summer and early autumn. For spring use, there is much to be said for the blue-flowering "Bluebell", the white *sibirica*, and the double white "White Moth" varieties of *C. alpina*; while for winter decoration, small sprays of *C. calycina* with their yellowish-white, spotted red flowers, and *C. cirrhosa*, with creamy-white downy flowers, are more interesting and valuable.

For the more colourful effect, however, the small-flowered varieties of the Viticella section are the most useful. They make delightful table decorations, particularly as they can be arranged low in height and spreading down the centre of a dining table, or drape and trail from tall vases, from the ends of shelves, mantelpieces or pedestal tables. Varieties worthy of special mention are "Little Nell", slaty mauve flowers in profusion; "Abundance", soft purple, beautifully veined; "Kermesina", bright red; "Minuet", cream-centred and banded purple; "Royal Velours", deep velvety purple; and *alba luxurians*, pearly white cup-like flowers.

One can look in vain in the florists' shops for sprays of Clematis, although if they are cut with a little of the older wood or stem attached to the base, with a slanting cut or slit, they last as well as any other comparable cut flower. It is also exceptional to find cut flowers of Clematis offered.

They order this matter differently in Holland, where the

lovely Lanuginosa hybrid "Prince Hendrick" is specially but gently forced for its very large, azure-blue flowers, with their fringed and wavy-margined sepals. With their strong stems, the flowers make excellent, long-lived cut blooms, lasting ten to fourteen days when arranged in water.

The flowers of other large-flowering hybrids can always be cut from the garden and brought indoors, though preference should be given to those producing a flower with a thickish stem; and where possible, they should be cut with a little of the older shoot attached.

Blooms of most kinds can be cut with short stems for use in shallow posy bowls, almost floating on the water. While this practice is deprecated in some quarters, they do make attractive centres for small tables, and allow us to enjoy the flowers indoors.

Varieties which lend themselves to cutting with long stems, sufficiently robust for composed arrangements, include "The President", its deep violet flowers fading seldom; "William Kennett", lavender, with crimped sepal margins; "Beauty of Worcester", bluish-violet with white stamens; and "Miriam Markham", lavender, of the Lanuginosa sections; "Edouard Desfosse", violet-mauve; and "La Lorraine", satin pink, tinged with blue, of the Patens section; and "Madame Edouard André", deep red; "Comtesse de Bouchaud", soft pink, tinted mauve; "Perle d'Azur", light blue; "Gipsy Queen", dark velvety purple; and "Madame Baron Veilliard", deep rose, of the Jackmanii section. "Huldine", the medium-sized flowering Viticella hybrid, is most charming for cutting, its white, translucent flowers, with the back of the sepals barred a mauve-pink, being produced in abundant clusters on long stems; while "Ernest Markham", a velvety petunia red, and "Etoile Violette", deep violet, are both distinctive, free-flowering related hybrids.

Much also can be made of the dark blue-violet flowers of *C.* x *durandii*, so freely produced throughout the summer.

Apart from their floral charms, several Clematis are of decorative worth for their plumose heads of seed vessels with long, silvery feathered styles, towards the end of the year.

*C. tangutica* is a most beautiful example, and may often be gathered accompanied by late yellow lanterns of flowers. Others which produce decorative seed heads are *C. flammula*, *C. alpina* and vars., *C. spooneri*, *C. quinquefoliolata*, and *C. chrysocoma*, while our native *C. vitalba* is outstanding for its silver-grey, tufted balls of plumose seeds, which, even out of doors last exceedingly long. Dried sprays of seed heads can be used to good effect in winter arrangements of other dried flowers and plants.

From these brief notes, it will be seen that Clematis in the garden can contribute unusual and decorative notes to the home indoors, all the more enticing since it is a field in which every Clematis grower can feel free to make his or her mark.

# *16*

## CLEMATIS IN OTHER COUNTRIES

*Because it climbs on lattice,*
*The rabble says Cle-mat'-is,*
*But Webster will not cease to hiss*
*Until they call it Clem'-a-tis.*

J. E. SPINGARN

THE HARDY garden Clematis discussed in this book are natives, or their varieties and hybrids, of the temperate regions of the world, and largely of the northern hemisphere. Their ability to grow well when transferred to countries other than their own is largely determined by the suitability of the climate, the soil and the plant environment. Their tolerance of temperatures is reasonably wide but not excessive, and the Clematis do not do well under hot semi-tropical or tropical conditions or in conditions which subject them to long spells of excessive cold. They are, however, adaptable to many types of soils provided these are supplied with lime, and succeed best in well-drained, humus-rich loams. Their particular environmental needs are a cool root run, and clear air with good light. With these facts in mind, it is useful to look at some of the countries in which Clematis have claimed their place in the affection of the gardener.

### AMERICA

Interest in the genus Clematis has never been quite so informed or so keen as in Britain and Western Europe, where America is concerned. The American continent, especially

*Clematis huldine.* Vigorous, upper surface white with pale mauve underneath. Flowers July-September.

*Clematis montana* in autumn, covered with its fluffy ornamental seed leaves.

if Canada be included, is one of wide climatic variation, and it is hardly to be expected that enthusiasm should be shown for these beautiful plants where too much heat in summer, too much cold in winter, and other factors limit their survival.

Nevertheless, in what might be termed the gardening regions of America, such as the states of the eastern and western sea-boards, and those of the temperate mid-west and south, many species, varieties and large-flowered hybrids of Clematis can be grown and successfully wintered.

Large-flowered Clematis have been grown in America since 1838, and interest in these was increasingly enlarged by the importation of large-flowering hybrids that resulted from the activities of such breeders as George Jackman and Son, Cripps and Son, C. Noble, and Anderson Henry in Britain, and Simon-Louis Frères, Victor Lemoine, Baron Veillard, and M. Späth in Europe, up to the end of the nineteenth century. Thereafter, interest fell away, until it was revived and fanned largely by the enthusiasm of one man, Mr. J. E. Spingarn of Troutbeck, Duchesse County, New York, whose apt verse heads this chapter with due acknowledgement. Today, there is a lively and keen interest in Clematis among American gardeners, and many of the species, with no less than fifty of the large-flowering hybrids, are worth growing.

The muted interest of American horticulturists in Clematis during the past century of their rising popularity elsewhere is rather curious in face of the fact that they can claim a number of species as natives. In this respect, North America is only out-rivalled by China and Eastern Asia.

There is, for instance, the delightful *C. texensis* with its distinctive, urn-shaped, thick-sepalled scarlet flowers, which is a native of Texas, but capable of surviving temperatures of fifteen to twenty degrees of frost, and of growing as far north as New England. A favourite in European gardens, it was crossed with a large-flowered Jackmanii hybrid, "Star of India", by George Jackman and Son in 1894 to give us "Countess of Onslow", the forerunner of several handsome and highly coloured hybrids such as "Duchess of York", "Duchess of Albany", "Admiration", and "Grace Darling", which do well wherever the parent *C. texensis* can be grown.

The deciduous *C. crispa*, with its bluish-purple, bell-shaped flowers of summer, grows wild in the states of the south, from Virginia to Texas, and is stated to be hardy enough to grow almost anywhere. The herbaceous *C. douglasii*, hailing from the north-western states of Wyoming, Washington and Montana, is hardy, and Mr. Spingarn links other western natives with it such as *C. columbiana*, *C. eriophora* and *C. pseudoalpina* which are not known in Europe.

*C. fremontii*, another herbaceous species, with a native background of Nebraska, Missouri, and Kansas, is perfectly hardy, and the spring-flowering climber *C. verticillaris* with its purplish blooms is found in eastern woods from North Carolina to Quebec. Others to which attention has been drawn include *C. versicolor*, a lavender flowering kind, native to Missouri and Arkansas; *C. pitcheri*, with purplish-blue, urn-shaped flowers; *C. viorna*, with reddish-purple, urn-shaped flowers in midsummer; and *C. virginiana*, with panicles of dull white flowers in late summer—all three being found in the eastern states of America.

Of species from elsewhere, the Japanese *C. paniculata* which bears its hawthorn-scented, white flowers in autumn, develops magnificently in the eastern states. Others which are grown with success in congenial soil and which can survive up to twenty and thirty degrees of frost include *C. montana* and its varieties, the Japanese *C. apiifolia*, *C. patens*, and its var. *grandiflora;* the Chinese *C. aethusifolia*, *C. chinensis*, *C. chrysocoma*, *C. fargesii*, *C. lanuginosa*, *C. spooneri*, *C. tangutica* and its var. *obtusiuscula*, and *C. uncinata;* and the Korean *C. koreana* and *C. serratifolia*. The Chinese species, *C. rehderiana* and *C. veitchiana*, and the evergreen *C. armandii* require winter protection further north than Philadelphia.

The European and British native, *C. vitalba*, survives without much protection in eastern states, and *C. viticella* can usually be grown without much difficulty. *C. alpina*, inured to a North European climate, transfers well to North America, at least as far north as Maine, and *C. macropetala*, which grows in

Siberia; *C. orientalis*, of northern Asia; and the herbaceous species, *C. recta*, *C.* x *eriostemon*, *C. heracleifolia*, *C. integrifolia*, *C. stans* and *C. ranunculoides* present little difficulty, surviving in the colder gardens with the help of winter mulches.

The New Zealand species, *C. afoliata* and *C. indivisa*, which are only hardy enough for warm sheltered gardens in England's southern counties, need the warmth of southern California and the Gulf States in America, where *C. meyeniana* of south-east China should also thrive. The evergreen *C. napaulensis* of Northern India, with its clusters of small silky, creamy-yellow flowers, having purple stamens, in winter and early spring would be enchanting for mild regions.

Turning to the large-flowered Clematis hybrids, no generalised principles can be laid down as to where they can and cannot be grown in so large and varied a continent as North America. They seem less able to stand up to dry, torrid, summer heat than to survive the winter cold. Consequently, they thrive less happily in states of the hot south, south-east and California than in the more northern and eastern states, but the large-flowered varieties of *C. texensis*, such as "Countess of Onslow", "Duchess of Albany", "Admiration", and "Grace Darling", often prove satisfactory.

Sight must not be lost of the fact that the Clematis genus is adapted to temperate conditions. While sunlight, preferably at least a six to eight-hour day, is essential to free flowering, the root system must be cool, moist and yet well drained. It is often possible to satisfy these conditions in areas where woodlands or shrubberies abound and where the elevation of the land gives a cooler climate than the average for a hot region.

The climate of the north-west states on the moister side of the Rockies, such as north California, Washington and as far north as Vancouver and lower British Columbia, resembles that of Britain sufficiently to make it possible to grow almost any of the large-flowered hybrids described in this book as hardy for Britain.

Another factor to be borne in mind is that Clematis, with few exceptions, like lime. This is important where it is desired to grow these lovely plants in the eastern seaboard states and those bordering the Canadian border. For the large-flowered hybrids, it is necessary to dress the acid soils so familiar to gardeners in the states of New York, New England, and Pennsylvania with ground limestone or chalk. Assured of lime, the range of large-flowered hybrids that can be grown is more extensive than is realised. Where winter conditions are apt to be severe, winter protection in the form of mulches with organic litter over the roots, will enable most of the hardy kinds to winter up to thirty degrees of frost.

American nurseries do not, however, offer Clematis in wide variety, and a short list of kinds likely to be obtainable and which experience has shown to be most likely to succeed is:

"Duchess of Edinburgh" and "*Sieboldii*" of the *C. florida* section.

"Comtesse de Bouchard", "Gipsy Queen", "Madame Edouard André", "Madame Baron-Veillard", "Mrs. Cholmondeley", and "The President" of the *C.* x *jackmanii* section, and *C.* x *jackmanii* itself.

"Beauty of Worcester", "Henryi", "Blue Gem", "Crimson King", "Lady Northcliffe", "Nelly Moser", "Prince Hendrick" and "Ramona" (known as *hybrida sieboldii* in Europe), of the *C. lanuginosa* section.

"Edouard Desfosse", "King of the Belgians", "La Lorraine", "Mrs. George Jackman", and "Sir Garnet Wolseley" of the *C. patens* section.

"Huldine", "Lady Betty Balfour", and "Ville de Lyon" of the large-flowering section of *C. viticella*.

Of these large-flowering hybrids, "Comtesse de Bouchard", "Gipsy Queen", "Henryi", "Ramona", "Huldine", and "Ville de Lyon" provide a safe and reliable nucleus for the beginner in America.

Of the smaller-flowering Clematis, besides the native species already mentioned, *C. alpina* and its varieties, *C. campaniflora*, *C.* x *jouiniana* and its varieties such as *praecox*, *C. orientalis*, and the small-flowering "Abundance", *alba luxurians*, *kermesina*, and "Royal Velours" of the *C. viticella* section, are excellent for a beginning. Where plants of species and their varieties are not available, they can often be obtained and raised from seed.

# Clematis in Other Countries

## AUSTRALIA

Although Clematis is not unknown in Australia—the country has its own native species which clambers in the bush in areas such as South Gippsland, but which does not seem to have been introduced to Britain—only a comparatively few kinds are cultivated to any extent. There does not seem any adequate reason for this. Anyone who has been in Victoria and New South Wales can testify to the Australians' love of flowers and gardening, though Clematis, especially the large-flowering hybrids, have yet to find a worthy place.

The aridity and climatic extremes plaguing so much of the Australian continent may deny the possibility of growing Clematis in many parts, but in the more temperate states, particularly of the south and west, the scope seems promising. The most popular and well-known Clematis here is *C. montana* and its varieties *grandiflora, rubens, undulata,* and *wilsonii,* to which might now be added "Elizabeth" and "Pink Perfection".

Where plants can be assured cool rooting conditions and lime in the soil there should be little difficulty in growing the species of China such as *C. armandii, C. chrysocoma, C. florida* and its var. *sieboldii, C. lanuginosa,* and *C. tangutica*; of Japan such as *C. patens*; and of America, such as *C. texensis*; while the Europeans *C. viticella, C. alpina, C. campaniflora* and *C. vitalba* should present no cultural difficulties in the cooler parts or hills, though the Australian gardener would probably find it necessary to make a start with such species from imported seeds.

The large-flowered hybrids, however, are chiefly grown in the public and botanical gardens, but the fact that they thrive in places such as Albury, New South Wales, and around Melbourne, indicates that they remain a promising source of beauty that the Australian gardener has yet to explore. Probably the greatest trial of Clematis hybrids in Australia is the long summer heat and light, but if grown in conjunction with shrubs or trees or in the light shade, they apparently succeed very well. The following are reported as being available in Victorian nurseries: "Belle of Woking", *C. florida* var. *sieboldii,*

"Lady Northcliffe", *lawsoniana*, "Mrs. Hope", "Nelly Moser", "Lasurstern", and "Ville de Lyon". Jackmanii and Viticella varieties are more scarce.

## CANADA

The areas in which Clematis may be grown in Canada are limited by the extremes of the climate, especially in winter. In the mild west of Columbia and the Vancouver region, where conditions are rather similar to those of England, species, varieties and hybrids hardy in Britain, can usually be grown without difficulty, though some lime amendment of the soil may be necessary.

Many species and varieties have, however, been grown successfully in the regions of the Great Lakes, on the limestone soil around Montreal, and experience suggests that, given some winter protection, even large-flowering hybrids such as "Henryi", "Madame Edouard André", "Mrs. George Jackman", "Nelly Moser", and "Ville de Lyon" can survive twenty degrees below zero. Where plants can be pot-grown and moved to the sheltered greenhouse for the winter, the scope is greatly increased. At present, hybridists in Canada are actively trying to evolve more hardy forms from varieties known to withstand the Canadian winter crossed with those of greater beauty. Those who already know of the work that Canadian hybridists have done in giving us finer Lilacs (*Syringa*) will watch their experiments with Clematis in expectant interest.

## NEW ZEALAND

In as much as New Zealand is the Britain of the antipodes both in national characteristics and climatic resemblance, there are no species, varieties or hybrids of Clematis grown in Britain that cannot be equally well, if not better grown, in New Zealand. New Zealand has also native species of its own, of which the vigorous evergreen *C. indivisa* and its variety *lobata*, with its almost unique (for the genus) unisexual white flowers, and *C. afoliata*, with its fragrant, greenish-white small flowers, are best known abroad.

This brief survey by no means concludes all the countries in which Clematis may be grown. Western Europe has shown an equal, and if anything, longer, interest in Clematis and their breeding than England. Portugal contributes a notably lovely deciduous climber in *C. campaniflora* which bears its bell-like, small, nodding, white, tinged violet flowers in summer. The Balearic Islands and Southern Europe are sources of the two winter-flowering evergreen climbers, *C. calycina* and *C. cirrhosa*, and from the south-east corners of Europe has come *C. viticella*, and the herbaceous species of *C. recta* and *C. integrifolia*. In France, Holland, and Belgium, nurserymen have played a part in the development of new varieties and hybrids, and the resources of the genus are by no means exhausted.

Of other countries, such as South Africa, where many Clematis are eligible for the cooler gardens of the Cape, and of countries of the Far East, little information of practical authority is available for these pages. But wherever in the world the conditions of climate, soil, and environment, come within the needs of the temperate needs of the genus, the challenge to grow Clematis is likely to be well worth taking up.

# 17

# A GLOSSARY OF GARDEN CLEMATIS

GLOSSARY, *n.* Partial dictionary.

*The Concise Oxford Dictionary*

THE HOPE behind this glossary is that it may serve as a ready and ever-helpful alphabetical reference to the Clematis species, varieties and hybrids at present available for garden cultivation.

In the endeavour to make it as up-to-date, informative and practical as possible, the plants are listed by their most appropriate names alphabetically. Species are included by their current botanical names and synonyms, followed by their varieties. Hybrids, however, especially the large-flowered types, are listed by the names given to them by their raisers and which are in common usage by nurserymen and growers.

Botanical nomenclature undergoes revision in Clematis as in other genera, and several species have thereby acquired synonyms. Where known, the synonyms have been included with cross-references to the current, and it is hoped, stable, present-day name. Common names have been given after the botanical names, where usage warrants, but have not been entered separately.

The country of origin and time of introduction into Britain have been included where possible. In the case of hybrids, notes on their breeding and their raisers have been given where ascertainable, though in many cases, no authentic information has come to light in my research.

In the case of varieties and hybrids listed by their everyday names, the following abbreviations have been used to indicate the group of Clematis to which they belong:

ALP.     *C. alpina* group.
ARM.    *C. armandii* group.
FLO.     *C. florida* group.
JAC.     *C.* x *jackmanii* group.
LAN.    *C. lanuginosa* group.
MAC.    *C. macropetala* group.
MON.    *C. montana* group.
PAT.    *C. patens* group.
TEX.     *C. texensis* group.
VIT. l-f.  *C. viticella*, large-flowering group.
VIT. s-f.  *C. viticella*, small-flowering group.

The designations D or E are used to indicate whether a plant is Deciduous or Evergreen, and notes of habit, form, vigour and height of growth must be taken as indications, as some latitude must be allowed according to the environment and soil in which plants may be grown. Flower colour and special garden features of the plants are given as accurately as possible, as well as indications on pruning and propagation, though fuller information on these points is set out in the chapters on these subjects.

ABUNDANCE. Hyb. VIT. s-f. Flowers small, soft purple, with distinct veining, freely produced from leaf axils.

*C. AETHUSIFOLIA.* Mongolia, Manchuria, 1855. D. Climber to 6 or 7 feet, with tri-foliate or pinnate leaves and deeply dissected leaflets, and pale yellow, small, bell-shaped, nodding, solitary flowers, on stiff, erect, 2–3 inch stalks, produced in ones to threes in the leaf axils. Rather elegant and pretty. Prune in early spring. Propagate by seeds, cuttings, layers.

*C. AFOLIATA.* (syn. *C. aphylla*). The Rush-stemmed C. New Zealand, 1908. D. A rather unusual shrubby climber, producing a mass of very slender, virtually leafless, dark green, drooping twigs, yellowing in autumn, and axillary clusters of two to six small greenish-white, inch-wide flowers, with 4–6 sepals, and diffusing a Mezereum fragrance, in May. Needs a sheltered south wall, and may not be fully hardy in exposed gardens. Pruning is difficult as the shoots interlace and tangle, but when necessary should be carried out in spring, immediately after flowering, by cutting back severely. Propagate by seeds, cuttings and layers.

*ALBA LUXURIANS.* Var. vɪᴛ. s-f Flowers small, pure pearly white, and cup-shaped, with dark stamens, freely produced from leaf axils, Aug.-Sept.

*C. ALPINA.* (Syn. *Atragene alpina.*) Alpine Virgin's Bower. A native of the mountains of central and northern Europe and north-east Asia. 1792. D. Climber to 6 or 8 feet, with long doubly ternate leaves, made up of coarsely toothed ovate leaflets, and solitary, four-sepalled, soft blue flowers, nodding on 3-inch stalks, in abundance in late April and May, and often a less profuse spatter of bloom again in late autumn. Spring flowers give way to fluffy, silky seed heads which are pretty in summer. Grows finely in a cool, north aspect. Prune young plants in February to form framework branches; thereafter in early August, shortening side shoots almost to their base. Propagate by seeds, cuttings and layers.

*C. ALPINA* var. *SIBIRICA.* (Syn. *C. a.* var. *alba.*) A pure white flowering variety of the above, more robust in growth, and flowering somewhat earlier in April. "Ruby" is a named selection, with single, nodding flowers of a soft rosy-red; and "White Moth" is a recent introduction with double flowers of pure white, and strong growth.

*C. APHYLLA.* Syn. of *C. afoliata* (Q.V.).

*C. APIIFOLIA.* Japan, 1869. D. Climber to 10 or 12 feet, with tri-foliate leaves of deeply toothed or lobed, ovate leaflets, and freely produced axillary panicles of dull white, small, four-sepalled flowers in late Aug.-Sept. Not often offered today. Prune in late winter. Propagate by seeds, cuttings and layers.

*C. ARMANDII.* Armand's Clematis, in honour of Père Armand David (1826–1900), French missionary in China. A native of central and southern China, introduced by E. H. Wilson, 1900. E. Climber, vigorous to 15 or 20 feet, impressive for its dark, glossy green, tri-foliate leaves, up to 6 inches long, and fragrant, pure white, four- to six-sepalled flowers, over 2 inches across, borne in clusters of threes from the leaf axils in April-May. "Apple Blossom" is a form bearing flowers that are tinged pink in the bud; but "Snowdrift", with clusters of larger pure white flowers in April, and large, leathery, pointed leaflets, is outstanding. Prune at the end of February, thinning out, and shortening lateral growths, with due regard to the fact that flowers come on the wood of the previous year. Propagate by seeds and layers. Hardy enough, except in exposed northern gardens, if given a warm, sheltered wall. In the south, can be grown on tripods, pillars or pergolas, or through trees with great effect.

C. *ARISTATA*. A native of south Australia and Tasmania. E. Climber, bearing small, four-sepalled white flowers freely in spring, followed by plumose seed heads. Only hardy for very sheltered gardens in the south. Prune February. Propagate by seeds or layers.

C. x *AROMATICA*. Hyb. *C. flammula* x *C. integrifolia*, originating about 1845. D. Herbaceous, with stems up to 6 feet, dying back to a woody rootstock, quin-foliate leaves, with entire, oval leaflets, and delightfully scented, dark blue flowers, up to 1½ inches across, freely produced in loose cymes from July to September. Well worth growing in the hardy plant border. Prune, if necessary, by cutting all growth to ground level early in the year. Propagate by seeds and by cuttings.

*ASCOTIENSIS*. Var. vit 1-f. Large flowers of bright, azure-blue, with pointed sepals, very freely produced in Aug.-Sept.

C. *AZUREA*. Syn. of *C. patens* (q.v.).

C. *BALEARICA*. Syn. of *C. calycina*, or *C. cirrhosa* (q.v.).

BARBARA DIBLEY. Hyb. PAT. Large flowers, after "Nelly Moser" for form, but of a deeper, rich pansy violet and deeper coloured bars, very freely borne, May-June.

BARBARA JACKMAN. Hyb. PAT. Large flowers of soft petunia, with distinct plum-coloured bars, and a centre of cream stamens, freely produced in May-June, and particularly recommended for a north or north-west aspect.

BARONNE DE VERDIERES. Hyb. PAT. Large flowers of lilac-rose, double, in May-June.

BEAUTY OF RICHMOND. Hyb. LAN. Flowers of most lovely shape, soft clear mauve with deeper bars, in June-July.

BEAUTY OF WORCESTER. Hyb. LAN. Flowers of deep bluish-violet, with a centre of prominent white stamens; double-flowering on old wood, single on young wood; in May-July, and often later.

BELLE NANTAISE. Hyb. LAN. Large flowers with long, pointed sepals of delicate greyish-lavender blue, freely produced in July-August.

BELLE OF WOKING. Hyb. FLO. Large double flowers of rosette shape, pale silvery-mauve, in May-June.

*C. BERGERONII.* Syn. of *C.* x *eriostemon* (q.v.)

BLUE BELLE. Hyb. LAN. Large single flowers of a dusky violet-blue, in July-Aug.

BLUE GEM. Hyb. LAN. Large single flowers of pale sky-blue, in July-Aug.

BRACEBRIDGE STAR. Hyb. JAC. Pennell, 1956. Large, star-like, eight-sepalled flowers, pointed, of lavender-blue, with carmine bar, in May-Sept.

*C. CALYCINA.* (Syn. *C. balearica.*) The fern-leaved C. A native of the Balearic Isles and southern Europe, introduced in 1783. E. Climber reaching 8 to 12 feet, with slender dark brown stems, ternate or doubly ternate leaves, with leaflets deeply lobed or toothed and fern-like, glabrous in summer, turning bronzy-purple in winter, and solitary, creamy-white, bell-shaped flowers, freckled red within, 1½ to 2 inches across, nodding on short stalks from the leaf axils in November-February. Valuable for its winter bloom, but somewhat tender, and needing shelter from chill winds or can be grown under glass. Prune after flowering. Propagate by seeds, cuttings, and layers.

*C. CAMPANIFLORA.* Portugal, 1820. D. Climber of 12 to 18 feet, with very slender stems, much divided, pinnate leaves, and small, nodding, widely spread, bell-shaped flowers, white, tinged bluish or violet, very freely produced, and effective in the mass, in July-Aug. Excellent for clothing arbours, sheds, or garden eye-sores, and for rambling through tall shrubs or small trees. Prune about February, cutting shoots back to their base. Propagate by seeds, cuttings and layers.

*C.* x *CHANDLERI.* Syn. of *C.* x *eriostemon* (q.v.).

*C. CHRYSOCOMA.* The Tufted or Hairy C. Found by Père Jean Marie Delavay (1834–1895), French missionary, in north-west Yunnan, China, in 1884, and introduced in Britain in 1910. D. Beautiful climber, vigorous up to 12 feet, with new shoots, leaves and stalks covered with dense, golden-brown down; leaves tri-foliate, with coarsely toothed or tri-lobed ovate leaflets, and four-sepalled flowers, up to 2 inches across, of white, tinged pink, on long stalks from the leaf axils, first appearing in June and then in succession on established plants until September. Grows easily in the open or on walls, with usual supports. Propagate by seeds, cuttings and layers. Prune in February, thinning out shoots, and bearing in mind that flowers are borne on the old wood.

*C. CHRYSOCOMA* var. *SERICEA.* Syn. of *C. spooneri* (q.v.).

*C. CIRRHOSA.* (Syn. *C. balearica* Persoon.) Winter-flowering C. Found on mountains of North Africa, Algeria, Spain, southern Europe and Asia Minor, introduced 1590. E. Climber, often confused with *C. calycina*, but less vigorous, growing 8 to 10 feet, with simple, ovate, coarsely toothed or tri-lobed, small ovate leaves, and solitary, pendulous, four-sepalled flowers, opening up to 2 inches wide, and creamy white, with a cup-like involucre behind the sepals, produced in mild weather during January to March. Esteemed for its winter flowers, but needs a sheltered corner or wall to show them well, or may be grown under glass. Propagate by seeds and layers. Prune after flowering, thinning out the shoots.

*C. COCCINEA.* Syn. of *C. texensis* (q.v.).

*C. COERULEA.* Syn. of *C. patens* (q.v.).

COMTESSE DE BOUCHAUD. Hyb. JAC. Flowers of medium size, saucer-shaped, of six sepals, a beautiful soft satiny pink, with a touch of mauve, very freely produced from June to October.

*C. CONNATA.* A native of the Himalaya and Chinese Border. 1880? D. Climber, described as vigorous to 20–25 feet, with large leaves, breaking into 3, 5, or 7 leaflets of ovate, pointed, coarsely toothed or lobed shape, and small, bell-shaped, fragrant, yellow flowers, of four sepals with tips reflexing, in panicles up to 5 inches long, from the leaf axils in autumn. Prune in February, rather severely. Propagate by seeds, cuttings and layers. Apparently not in general cultivation.

*C. CORDATA.* Syn. of *C. pitcheri* (q.v.).

COUNTESS OF LOVELACE. Hyb. FLO. Raised by G. Jackman, Woking, 1872. Delightful for its violet-blue, double flowers, composed of an outer row of guard sepals, and a centre rosette of smaller ones; produced from the previous year's growth in June.

COUNTESS OF ONSLOW. Hyb. TEX. Bell-or Hyacinth-shaped flowers of a bright violet-purple, with a scarlet band down each sepal, freely produced, July-Sept.

CRIMSON KING. Hyb. LAN. Probably the best crimson large-flowered C, with bright rosy-red sepals, paling down the centre, and a centre boss of yellow-brown stamens, very free, July-Aug.

*C. CRISPA.* South-east U.S.A., 1726. The Frilled or Marsh C. D. Semi-woody climber of 8 to 10 feet, slender and delicate, often dying back to near ground level in winter; furnished with 3, 5, or 7 pinnate leaves, made up of thin, ovate leaflets, and solitary, bell-shaped, fragrant, bluish-purple flowers, with wavy-margined sepals up to 2 inches long, on 3-inch stalks, June-Aug., successionally. A light, graceful plant for borders, pruning consisting of cutting previous year's growth to base in early spring. Propagate by seeds or root division. Var. *distorta* is seldom seen, but varies in the sepals tending to curl.

DANIEL DERONDA. Hyb. PAT. Large purple-blue flowers, with a centre of yellow stamens, and pointed sepals, which are semi-double from the previous year's shoots in May, followed by more single flowers later, and flowering into July.

*C. DAVIDIANA.* Syn. of *C. heracleifolia* var. *davidiana* (q.v.).

DUCHESS OF ALBANY. Hyb. TEX. Hyacinth, bell-shaped flowers of a bright pink, July-Sept.

DUCHESS OF EDINBURGH. Hyb. FLO. One of the best large-flowering, pure white double types, flowers of rosette formation, sweetly scented. May-June.

DUCHESS OF SUTHERLAND. Hyb. VIT l-f. Large, bright red flowers with a lighter bar; double and then single, Aug.-Oct.

DUCHESS OF YORK. Hyb. TEX. Bell-shaped flowers of deep pink, paling at the margins of the fleshly sepals.

DUKE OF PORTLAND. Hyb. LAN. Large flowers of pale pink, with crimson bars, May: July-Oct.

*C. DOUGLASII.* Montana, Wyoming and Washington States of U.S.A., 1889. Herbaceous, with stems, 1 to 2 feet tall, pinnate foliage of narrow linear leaflets, and solitary nodding flowers, purple, with oblong, pointed sepals, 1½ inches long, gracefully borne on stout woolly stalks, in May-June. Propagate by seeds or by root division in spring. Discovered by, and named after, David Douglas.

*C. x DURANDII.* Hyb. *C. integrifolia* x *C. x jackmanii*, Lyons, France, 1870. D. Climber up to 6 or 8 feet, with stems more or less dying back in winter; simple, entire, ovate, glabrous leaves, 4 to 6 inches long on shorter stalks, with most pleasing flowers of four or more, wavy-margined sepals of dark violet-blue, up to 4½ inches across, with yellow stamens, freely borne from June to September. In var. *pallida*, the flowers are of a paler violet, tinged with rose. Both kinds are among the easiest Clematis to grow, in borders, or up fences or pillars. Prune by cutting previous year's growth back 2 to 3 feet from the ground. Propagate by cuttings in late spring, or by root division in February.

EDOUARD DESFOSSE. Hyb. PAT. Flowers exceptionally large, sometimes inches across, made up of six or more pointed sepals of violet-mauve, with darker bars, in May—the earliest flowering of the Patens hybrids.

ELSA SPATH. Hyb. LAN. Large, single flowers of bright blue with darker tone towards the centre, July-Aug.

EMPRESS OF INDIA. Hyb. LAN. Impressive flowers of light violet-purple, deepening to the centre, down the sepals, and a central rosette of brown stamens, July-Aug.

ENCHANTRESS. Hyb. FLO. Beautiful, large, semi-double white flowers, late May-June.

C. ERECTA. Syn. of C. recta (q.v.).

C. x ERIOSTEMON. (Syns. C. bergeronii, C. chandleri, C. x hendersonii, C. x intermedia.) Hyb. C. integrifolia x C. viticella, raised by a Mr. Henderson, St. John's Wood, London, about 1820. Herbaceous climber, with slender shoots to 8 feet, with simple then pinnate leaves of ovate, entire leaflets up the shoots, and solitary, scented, rich deep blue flowers, made up of four sepals, spreading 2 to 3 inches across, on 3 to 4-inch stalks, produced profusely for a long period of July to Sept. Excellent in all situations where a plant of moderate growth is wanted. The shoots die back and can be cleared at soil level in winter. Propagate by cuttings and root division.

ERNEST MARKHAM. Hyb. VIT. l-f. Large flowers of a glowing petunia red, borne freely, July-Sept. Raised by Ernest Markham, at Gravetye, 1926.

ETOILE DE PARIS. Hyb. PAT. Large flowers of violet ground with white centre, May-July.

ETOILE VIOLETTE. Hyb. VIT. s-f. Attractive medium-sized flowers of deep violet colour, with yellow stamens in pleasant contrast, very freely borne, July-Aug.

FAIR ROSAMUND. Hyb. PAT. raised G. Jackman, 1870. Large, star-like flowers, with eight, oblong, pointed sepals, blush-white, with pale wine-red bar down the centre, and purple-red stamens, May-June.

FAIRY QUEEN. Hyb. LAN. Very large flowers of a pale pink, with a deeper pink bar down each sepal in the middle, July-Aug.

*C. FARGESII*. A native of China, named for Père Paul Farges (1844–1912), French missionary, Szechwan, introduced in Britain 1911. D. Climber of vigour to 20 feet, with purplish, hairy young shoots, doubly ternate leaves, with ovate, pointed, toothed leaflets, and pure white flowers of six obovate sepals, 2 to 3 inches across, borne singly or in small numbers on long axillary stalks, successively from June into the autumn. Prune to thin the shoots in Feb.-March. Propagate by seeds, cuttings and layers.

*C. FLAMMULA*. The Fragrant Virgin's Bower, or Sweet-scented C. D. Semi-woody climber of luxuriant growth, introduced from southern Europe in 1590. Vigorous to 12 or 15 feet, with variable divided leaves of entire, glabrous, lanceolate leaflets,

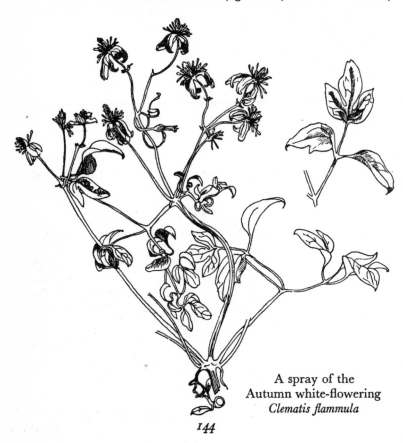

A spray of the
Autumn white-flowering
*Clematis flammula*

Clematis. The President. A vigorous grower with
6-7″ flowers of light purple. Anthers reddish-purple.
Flowers May-October.

Clematis Ville de Lyon. Flowers twice between late
May and September. A vigorous grower to 12 feet.

*Clematis macropetala*. A vigorous climber to 15 feet. Flowers April-May and sometimes in autumn.

and valuable for its richly scented, small inch-wide flowers, of four sepals with a centre of crowded white stamens, freely produced in loose, branching panicles in late summer and autumn, diffusing a sweet, hawthorn-like fragrance. Silky, silvery-grey seed heads succeed the flowers. Ideal for rambling over evergreen trees, or fences. Prune by cutting previous year's growth back to base in early spring. Propagate by seeds, cuttings and layers.

C. *FLORIDA*. China. 1776. D., sometimes partly E. Slender and fragile climber of 8 to 12 feet, with variable ternate or double ternate leaves, made up of small ovate or lanceolate leaflets, and solitary flowers, of four to six sepals, creamy-white with a greenish stripe down the back, up to 3 inches wide, on stalks 4 inches long, in June-July. Several varieties have occurred, but those chiefly offered are var. *flore pleno*, double-flowering, with white staminodes in the centre, and var. *sieboldii* (syn. *bicolor*), introduced from Japan in 1837, and the most striking, with the centre of the flower made up of a rosette of purple staminoides. Although eligible for sheltered walls, fences, etc., out of doors, these plants are most appreciated under glass. *C. florida* is also one of the parents of several large-flowered hybrid garden Clematis, which begin flowering from the old or ripened wood of the previous year's growth in early summer, and usually bear double or semi-double flowers. The finest varieties now in cultivation include "Bell of Woking", "Countess of Lovelace", "Duchess of Edinburgh", "Enchantress", "Mme. Alfred Bonneau", "Proteus", "Lucie Lemoine", "Undine", and "Ville de Limoges", described under their individual entries. Prune species, varieties and hybrids as soon as flowers are over, by cutting their shoots back severely, treating about half of the shoots in each year; and go over in January-February to remove dead or weak growth. Propagate species by seeds; cuttings and layers; varieties and hybrids by cuttings, layers and, when required, by grafts.

C. *FORRESTII*. Syn. of *C. napaulensis* (q.v.).

C. *FREMONTII*. Kansas, Missouri, and Nebraska states of U.S.A., 1880? Herbaceous, with stout, woolly, erect stems, 1 to 2 feet high, with ovate, more or less entire, leathery leaves, stalkless, heavily veined, and up to 4 inches long, and small, drooping, hyacinth-shaped, purplish flowers, with thick sepals, recurving at the tips, at the tops of the stems in July-August.

More of botanical interest than of garden beauty. Propagate by seeds and root division.

*C. FUSCA.* Manchuria and north-east Asia. 1860. D. Sub-shrubby climber, with stems tending to die back in winter, growing 8 feet or more with support; pinnate leaves with 5 or 7 ovate, entire, leaflets, 1½ to 2½ inches long, and small, urn-shaped, solitary flowers, reddish-brown and covered with hair on the outside, violet within, on short, stout, hairy stalks in June, followed by thick, round heads of plumose seeds later. A distinctive plant for the back of flower borders, or may be planted where the stems can lie and hang over a rock wall. Prune in Feb., cutting back to living wood. Propagate by seeds.

GIPSY QUEEN. Hyb. JAC. Large flowers of dark, rich violet-purple with a velvety sheen, star-like shape, in July-Aug.

*C. GLAUCA.* Western China and Siberia. 1752. D. Climber of slender stems, reaching to 10 feet, with pinnate or double-pinnate leaves, made up of small, bi- or tri-lobed, very glaucous leaflets, and orange-yellow flowers, up to 2 inches across, on slender axillary stalks in late summer and autumn. Its var. *akebioides,* introduced from western China in 1904, flowers somewhat earlier, with deep orange-yellow flowers, scented, often followed by silvery seed heads, and makes a lovely garden variety for clambering over rocks, tree stumps or walls. Prune to thin in February. Propagate from suckers, or by seeds and layers.

GLOIRE DE ST. JULIEN. Hyb. LAN. Fine large white flowers, suffused white, June-Sept.

GRACE DARLING. Hyb. TEX. Very lovely pitcher-shaped flowers of a bright rosy-carmine, freely produced, July-Sept.

GRAND DUCHESS. Hyb. LAN. Large blush-white flowers freely produced, July-Oct.

*C. GRACILIFLORA.* China. 1910. D. Climber up to 14 feet, with downy young shoots, ternate or pinnate leaves made up of small, coarsely toothed or lobed, ovate leaflets, and white, four-sepalled, cross-like flowers, 2 inches across, born in twos or fours from the leaf axils on slender stalks, in June. Resembles *C. chrysocoma* in its habit and charm. Prune in February, thinning out the shoots. Propagate by seeds, cuttings and layers.

*C. GRATA.* A native of the Indian Himalaya, but difficult to find in cultivation. D. Climber of vigour to 20 or 30 feet, with five-leafleted leaves, and small, one-inch diameter, four- or five-sepalled, creamy-white flowers, borne in terminal and axillary panicles of threes, attractively scented, in Sept.-Oct. Var. *grandidentata* (syn. *argentilucida*) was introduced from China in 1907, with tri-foliate leaves, with few large teeth, and downy on both sides; and white, sweet-scented flowers more freely produced than in the type, and much earlier in April-June, followed by silky shining seed heads. As a vigorous climber, it is best rambling through and over large shrubs or small trees in a wild garden, needing little pruning. Propagate by seeds, cuttings and layers.

*C. GRAVEOLENS.* Syn. of *C. orientalis* (q.v.).

GRAVETYE BEAUTY. Hyb. TEX. Flowers of a rich deep red, with sepals more open than is usual in this group, July-Sept.

GRAVETYE VARIETY. A form of *C. tangutica* (q.v.).

GUIDING STAR. Hyb. JAC. Large flowers of a purple ground, shaded crimson, in July-Oct.

HAGLEY HYBRID. Hyb. LAN. Large flowers of deep shell-pink, with centre of dark-brown stamens; raised by Percy Picton, introduced by J. Fisk, 1956; blooming June-Sept.

*C. x HENDERSONII.* Syn. of *C. x eriostemon* (q.v.).

HENRYI. Hyb. LAN. Large, beautiful white flowers, with long, pointed sepals and a centre of dark stamens, June-July.

*C. HERACLEIFOLIA.* (Syn. *C. tubulosa.*) North China and Mongolia. 1837. D. Sub-shrub with herbaceous stems of 3 to 4 feet, rather coarse tri-foliate leaves, with central leaflet much bigger than the other two, and hyacinth-like, tubular, small blue flowers, with reflexed sepal tips, in short, dense axillary clusters, spreading a sweet fragrance in Aug.-Sept. Var. *davidiana* (syn. *C. davidiana*), introduced from China by l'Abbe David (1826–1900), French missionary, in 1864, grows taller, and bears flowers with longer, unreflexed sepals of a deeper indigo-blue, with the sexes on different plants; those of the male being slightly larger. Both type and variety are good border plants. The old growth is removed to the base each winter. Propagate by seeds, cuttings and root division.

HULDINE. Hyb. VIT. l-f. Distinctive flowers of a pearly bluish-white and semi-translucent, with a mauve-pink bar down its sepal on the reverse side, abundantly produced, July-Sept. A Clematis to be trained above eye-level, so that the beauty of its blossoms can be seen against a sunny sky.

*C. INDIVISA.* Introduced from New Zealand, 1840. E. Climber of vigour, with downy, ribbed shoots to 8 or 10 feet, and tri-foliate leaves, made up of ovate, blunt-ended leaflets of 2 to 3 inches long. The flowers, made up of pure white sepals, six to eight in number, with yellow stamens and pink anthers measure 2 to 3 inches across, and are very freely borne in axillary panicles, in May-June. They are unisexual, and male plants carry the larger flowers. Var. *lobata* is equally pretty, with leaves coarsely toothed or lobed, and flowers larger than in the type. The plants are somewhat tender, though hardy enough for sheltered gardens in the south-west counties of England. Elsewhere, it needs protection or should be grown under glass, being a fine variety for cool greenhouses.

*Clematis heracleifolia*

*C. INTEGRIFOLIA*. A native of southern Europe, introduced in 1573. Herbaceous perennial with semi-woody stock, growing stems erect to 2 to 3 feet, with simple, entire, pointed, ovate leaves, and solitary, bell-shaped, nodding, velvety blue flowers, with fleshy sepals, on 1½-inch stalks, produced in clusters towards the end of the stems in July. There are violet and white forms. Prune by removing old stems in winter. Propagate by seeds or root division.

*C.* x *INTERMEDIA*. Syn. of *C.* x *eriostemon* (q.v.).

*C.* x *JACKMANII*. Hyb. *C. lanuginosa* x *C. viticella* x *C.* x *eriostemon*, by G. Jackman & Sons, 1858. D. Climber, with stems to 8 to 12 feet, leaves simple or tri-foliate, and large, rich violet-purple flowers, up to 5 inches across, made up of four to six sepals, exquisitely veined, and freely produced, in threes usually, from leaf axils from July to October. The original and best known type of the large-flowered garden Clematis, excellent for walls, porches, growing through trees, and all conceivable garden uses. Var. *alba*, raised by C. Noble, 1878, is a further Hyb of *C. patens* var. *alba* x *C.* x *jackmanii*, and is of separate distinction in that the flowers are double and white at first, then single flowers are produced later in the flowering season. Var. *rubra* bears flowers of a good deep red; and var. *superba* is an improved form of the original hybrid, with flowers of a dark violet-purple and broader sepals. Then there are the named selections: "Comtesse de Bouchaud", "Bracebridge Star", "Gipsy Queen", "Guiding Star", "Madame Edouard André", "Madame Baron-Veillard", "Magnifica", "Mrs. Cholmondeley", "Perle d'Azur", "Rubella", "Star of India", "The President", "Velutina purpurea", and "Victoria", which are described under their own names.

These plants flower from the growth of the current season, and are pruned by cutting hard back after flowering to above a node about 6 inches from the base of the year's growth. In the case of var. *alba*, however, growth should be thinned only, and the lateral shoots pruned back to their base, in order to preserve a sequence of double, then single flowers in the blossom period. Propagate by cuttings and layers.

*C.* x *JEUNEANA*. Hyb. *C. armandii* x *C. pavoliniana*. 1914. E. Vigorous climbing hybrid of two evergreen Chinese species, growing up to 20 feet, with character and foliage resembling that of its first parent, but remarkable for its small, inch-wide flowers, made up of five or six white sepals, pink on the reverse, in clusters of several cymes of three to five flowers, produced from the leaf axils in March-April. Because of its early flowering, it deserves a warm sheltered wall, or can be grown in a conservatory. Prune towards the end of January, thinning out shoots and shortening laterals, with the knowledge that flowers are borne of the previous year's wood. Propagate by cuttings and layers. Unfortunately, rather hard to obtain.

*C.* x *JOUINIANA*. Hyb. *C. heracleifolia* v. *davidiana* x *C. vitalba*. 1900. D. A vigorous and highly ornamental climber to 12 feet, with tri- or quin-foliate leaves of ovate, coarsely toothed leaflets up to 4 inches long, and small, four-sepalled, whitish to pale lilac-blue, hyacinth flowers which are borne in corymbs from leaf axils and ends of shoots to make panicles of 2 to 4 feet long, Aug.-Oct. Seen to best advantage when grown over a small tree or pergola where the shoots can cascade over, and trail. Also good for covering tree stumps, and garden eye-sores. Var. *praecox* has flowers of soft lavender-blue. Prune in February, thinning out shoots, and cutting back the older stems from time to time to encourage new growth. Propagate by cuttings, and can be raised from seeds, though seedlings show variation.

*KERMESINA*. Var. vit. s-f. Attractive for its small, bright red flowers, produced freely, July-Sept. See *C. vitacella*.

*C. KOREANA.* (Syn. *Atragene koreana.*) Korean Clematis, introduced 1820. Described as a decumbent shrub with stems slender and tending to grow prostrate, though they can be trained to climb. D. with tri-foliate leaves of coarsely toothed, cordate-ovate leaflets, 2 to 3½ inches long, bearing solitary, nodding flowers, reddish to dull violet, with reflexing sepals, and opening to about 1½ inches across, on stalks up to 6 inches long, from June into summer. Var. *lutea* has yellow flowers. The plants have an appealing elegance, but are not often listed. Prune rather hard in February. Propagate by seeds and cuttings.

KING EDWARD VII. Hyb. lan. Large handsome flowers of a purplish-violet or rose, with a soft crimson bar down the middle of each sepal, June-Oct.

KING GEORGE V. Hyb. vit. l-f. Flowers of pale flesh pink with a bright pink bar down the middle of each sepal, freely produced. July-Oct.

KING OF THE BELGIANS. Hyb. pat. Flowers of lavender-mauve,

with a bar of deeper colour down the middle of each sepal, May-July.

LADY BETTY BALFOUR. Hyb. VIT. l-f. Flowers of deep rich violet-blue, offset by yellow stamens, very freely produced, Sept.-Oct.

LADY CAROLINE NEVILLE. Hyb. LAN. Raised by Cripps and Son, Tunbridge Wells, 1866. Large flowers, six sepalled, of pale clear mauve, with deeper coloured bar down the middle of each sepal, and anthers of a pale reddish-brown on white filaments, June to October.

LADY LONDESBOROUGH. Hyb. PAT. Raised by C. Noble, Sunningdale, 1869. Flowers of a delicate pale mauve or silvery grey, with lighter bar down the middle of the sepals, and chocolate-purple anthers, May-June.

LADY NORTHCLIFFE. Hyb. LAN. Large flowers of a lovely deep lavender-blue, tinted bright blue, with purple at the base of the sepals, and attractive white stamens, June-Oct.

LA FRANCE. Hyb. LAN. Large flowers of rich deep violet-purple, with brown anthers, June-Oct.

LA LORRAINE. Hyb. PAT. Flowers of a satin-pink, diffused with blue, May-June.

C. LANUGINOSA. Great-flowered Virgin's Bower, woolly-leaved Clematis, Introduced from China, by Robert Fortune, about 1850. D. Climber with stems to 6 to 9 feet, furnished with simple or tri-foliate leaves, with leaflets of broad, ovate pointed shape, up to 5 inches long, on long stalks, and woolly beneath, and large flowers, up to 6 inches across, of six to eight, overlapping sepals, pale lavender to pale lilac, and a centre of reddish-brown anthers, freely born in ones to threes, June-Oct. There are a number of varieties such as var. *alba magna*, bearing white flowers with very broad sepals; var. *candida*, with flowers of a greyish white, which is a hybrid form (*C. lanuginosa* x *C. patens*); var. *pallida*, a form with larger but paler flowers than the type from Japan, and seldom seen today. The species is of greatest significance as the parent of many large-flowered garden hybrids, and has been crossed with several other species, including *C. florida* and *C. patens*. Among the most desirable hybrids of the Lanuginosa group are: "Beauty of Worcester", "Belle Nantaise", "Blue Gem", "Crimson King", "Duke of Portland", "Elsa Spath", "Empress of India", "Fairy Queen", "Gloire de St. Julien", "Grand Duchess", "Henryi", "King Edward VII", "Lady Caroline Neville", "Lady Northcliff",

"La France", "Lawsoniana", "Lord Neville", "Madame le Coultre", "Madame van Houtte", "Marie Boisselot", "Miriam Markham", "Mrs. Bush", "Mrs. Cholmondeley", "Mrs. Hope", "Otto Froebel", "Prince Hendrick", "Princess of Wales", "Queen Alexandra", "Robert Hanbury", "Sensation", "W. E. Gladstone", and "William Kennet".

There is usually a first flush of flowers in June or early July, and then a pause, when after a few weeks, flowering begins again and succeeds into the autumn. There are two ways of pruning. Either the plants can be trained to form a framework of branches, with the side branches being cut fairly hard back in late summer, to give early bloom from the last year's shortened growth, or all growth can be cut back annually in winter, before the end of January, to within 12 or 18 inches of the ground, and the new shoots will give somewhat later but larger and more abundant flowers. Propagate species by seeds, cuttings and layers; varieties and hybrids by cuttings and layers when true-to-type plants are required. Seeds are often produced from all kinds, however, and if sown will offer the prospect of interesting and possibly exceptional seedlings.

*C. LASIANDRA.* Introduced from China in 1900. D. Climber to 15 feet, with large ternate or bi-ternate leaves, and coarsely toothed, ovate leaflets, and small, bell-shaped, dull purple flowers, produced from leaf axils in ones to threes, in October. Is seldom listed or seen, as flowering is too dull and too late in the year to be greatly desired.

LASURSTERN. Hyb. PAT. V. Large flowers of deep purple-blue, in May-June from old wood, and often in Aug.-Sept. from young wood.

*LAWSONIANA.* Hyb. LAN. Raised by Mr. Anderson-Henry from *C. lanuginosa* x *C. patens* var. *fortunei*, 1870. Flowers are very large, clear sky-blue, flushed mauve, June-Oct.

LE CID. Hyb. PAT. Large flowers of clear lilac-mauve, June-Oct. Dropping out of English lists.

*C. LIGUSTICIFOLIA.* A native of the western states of U.S.A., introduced to Britain in 1880, but not often offered today. D. Climber, growing vigorously to 20 feet or more, with pinnate leaves, made up of five or seven coarsely toothed, ovate, glabrous leaflets, and unisexual flowers which are small, white, fragrant and borne in terminal and axillary panicles, in Sept. Var. *californica*, native to eastern U.S.A., differs in its leaves being velvety with down underneath, a characteristic plant adaptation to a hotter clime.

LITTLE NELL. Hyb. VIT. s-f. Produces small, 1½ to 2 inches across, flowers of a delicate slate-mauve, very freely in July-Sept.

LORD GIFFORD. Hyb. PAT. Flowers of rosy-purple, May-Sept.

LORD NEVILLE. Hyb. LAN. Large flowers of dark plum-purple, with a deeper bar down the centre of the sepals, which have a wavy edge, June-Aug.

LUCIE LEMOINE. Hyb. FLO. Raised by M. Victor Lemoine, Nancy, France, 1869. Flowers large, to five inches across, double, with many sepals of pure white, set off by a central tuft of primrose-yellow stamens, July-Aug. A very good double flower.

*C. MACROPETALA.* (Syn. *Atragene macropetala.*) A graceful native of China and Siberia, introduced in 1910 by Reginald Farrer from Kansu to Britain, though it had been collected some eighty years previously by a Russian botanist, Ilia Kuznetsov, and even earlier by the French missionary and botanist, Pierre Nicholas le Chèron D'Incarville (1706–1757) who found it in north China in 1742. It is sometimes called the Downy Clematis. D. A slender, but free and vigorous climber to 10 to 12 feet, producing shoots at an angle, which are downy, and furnished with doubly ternate leaves, of ovate, coarsely toothed, 1 to 1½ inches long, and delightful solitary flowers made up of a double row of pointed sepals, with an inner ring of petaloid staminoides characteristic of the Atragene group, from 2½ to 4 inches across, and a soft shade of lavender or violet-blue, in May-June, and often again in the autumn. Seedlings are variable, but there is a fine form in "Markham's Pink" (syn. *C. macropetala* var. *markhamii*), with flowers of a lovely clear pink, raised by the late Ernest Markham, who did much to bring Clematis to the fore. "Lagoon" is a recent introduction with medium blue flowers. Prune in winter, before March, cutting out weak shoots and shortening others. Propagate by seeds, cuttings and layers.

MADAME ALFRED BONNEAU. Hyb. FLO. Large, semi-double flowers of satiny-rose and white, from June onwards.

MADAME BARON-VEILLARD. Hyb. JAC. Large, lilac-rose flowers appearing rather late in July.

MADAME EDOUARD ANDRÉ. Hyb. JAC. A fine form, producing its medium-sized, bright, deep, velvety-red flowers with yellow stamens and pointed sepals freely in July-Aug.

MADAME GRANGE. Hyb. VIT. l-f. Flower of crimson-violet, with a red bar down the middle of each sepal, July-Sept.

MADAME JULES CORREVON. Flowers of a somewhat plummy-red, July-Sept. Hyb. VIT. l-f.

MADAME LE COULTRE. Hyb. LAN. Large white flowers, produced freely, May to September.

MADAME VAN HOUTTE. Hyb. LAN. Introduced in 1867 but disappearing from catalogues, although its very large, fine white flowers are of high quality and freely produced May-Sept.

MAGNIFICA. Hyb. JAC. An early form, now neglected and disappearing, freely producing flowers of a rich, reddish-purple, with a three-ribbed bar of crimson down each sepal, and pale brown anthers, July-Sept.

MARCEL MOSER. Hyb. PAT. Large flowers, with long pointed sepals of a soft mauve-velvet, with a deep carmine bar down the middle, May-June.

MARIE BOISSELOT. Hyb. LAN. Full large flowers with rounded sepals of pure white, with a centre of yellow stamens, June-Aug.

MARKHAM'S PINK. See *Clematis macropetala.*

MATHIEU DE DOMBASLE. Hyb. VIT. l-f. Double flowers of violet-mauve, July-Sept.

*C. MEYENIANA.* A native of south-eastern China, introduced from Macao in 1820, and named after the German, Franz T. J. Meyen (1804–40). E. Climber, resembling *C. armandii*, with which it hybridises readily, but with narrower and smaller leaves, somewhat smaller flowers with five to seven pointed sepals, and a sweet, orange-blossom-like scent, as early as February or March. May be grown out of doors in sheltered gardens of the south and west, on warm walls, attaining to 20 feet, but is better as a cold greenhouse plant elsewhere. Flowers are borne on the wood of the previous year, but pruning is most conveniently done in winter, thinning out growths only. Propagate by seeds and layers.

MINUET. Hyb. VIT. s-f. A delightful, distinctive, small-flowering form, producing cream-centred flowers, with a broad band of purple to the ends of the sepals, very freely, Aug-Sept.

MIRIAM MARKHAM. Hyb. LAN. Large flowers of a deep lavender, produced double on the older wood in May-June, and single on the young wood until Aug.

MISS BATEMAN. Hyb. PAT. Large, star-shaped, broad-petalled white flowers, with chocolate-red stamens in the centre, May-June.

MISS CRAWSHAY. Hyb. LAN. A beautiful pink flowering form, with yellow stamens, June-Aug.

M. KOSTER. Hyb. VIT. s-f. With soft, rosy-pink, medium-sized flowers, most abundantly produced, this makes a mass of bloom of great effect, July-Aug.

MRS. BUSH. Hyb. LAN. Large flowers of a clear, deep lavender-blue, May-Sept.

MRS. CHOLMONDELEY. Hyb. LAN. Large flowers of light blue, with longish, narrow and reflexed sepals, very freely produced, May-Sept.

MRS. GEORGE JACKMAN. Hyb. PAT. Large, satiny-white flowers, with a cream bar down the middle of the sepals, and dark brown stamens, May-June.

MRS. HOPE. Hyb. LAN. Large flowers of satiny mauve, with a bar of deeper colour down the middle of the sepals, and white stamens, July-Aug.

MRS. P. B. TRAUX. Hyb. PAT. Large flowers of periwinkle-blue, and yellow stamens, June-Aug.

MRS. SPENCER CASTLE. Hyb. VIT. l-f. Pale pinkish heliotrope flowers which are double on the old wood, single on the young, June-Oct.

MODESTA. Hyb. VIT. l-f. Clear violet flowers, June-Sept.

C. *MONTANA.* The White, or Great Indian Virgin's Bower. Introduced in 1831 from the Himalaya by Countess Amherst (1803-38). D. Vigorous climber of 20 to 30 feet, with ternate leaves of toothed, pointed, ovate leaflets, 2 to 4 inches long, and pure white flowers, 2 to 2½ inches across, sweet-scented, and consisting of four oval sepals, borne singly on stalks of 2 to 5 inches, in clusters of two to five from the leaf axils, with great freedom from May to June. The flowers have been compared to those of the wild wood anemone. A plant will cover a wall to a height of 40 feet or more, but can also be used on pergolas, fences, and to grow through old trees where there is ample space for development. To curtail it to smaller spaces, it must be pruned rather severely. There are several improved forms. Var. *grandiflora* has much larger flowers, up to 3¼ inches across, and blooms slightly earlier; var. *lilacina* has flowers flushed with a bluish-lilac; var. *rubens* is a Chinese variety, with purplish leaves when young, and beautiful rosy-red flowers in June, and from which has been developed "Elizabeth" a form with fragrant soft pink flowers, and "Pink Perfection", a form with deep pink flowers; and var. *wilsonii*, another Chinese variety which bears large white flowers, 3 inches across, distinctive for their attractively twisted sepals, in June-August. Ideally, pruning should be carried out when flowering is over, in July or August, as flowers are borne on wood of the previous year's growth. Shoots intended to form framework branches are trained in their places, and lateral shoots shortened to within reach of their base. A more rough and ready method, often more convenient with older plants, is to defer pruning until winter, and simply thin out the shoots, and shorten others to fit the space available. Propagate by seeds, but only retain worthy seedlings; by cuttings and layers for plants true to type.

*C. NAPAULENSIS.* (Syn. *C. forrestii*.) A native of North India and China, introduced into Britain in 1912. E. Vigorous climber up to 30 feet, with tri- or quin-foliate leaves, which starts into new growth each year in winter, carrying its singular flowers on stalks, in axillary clusters of up to eight or ten; each flower made up of four, creamy-yellow, silky, ovate sepals, about an inch long, and a centre of purple stamens. They appear in winter and early spring, and the plant should be given a sheltered south-west wall in southern counties, but is happiest under glass in colder localities. Prune in December, thinning out the weak and excess shoots. Propagate by cuttings and layers.

NELLY MOSER. Hyb. PAT. Very beautiful pale mauve-pink flowers, with a deep carmine bar down the sepals, freely produced, May-June and again in September.

*C. NUTANS, C. NUTANS THYRSOIDES.* Synonyms of *C. rehderiana* (q.v.).

*C. ORIENTALIS.* (Syn. *C. graveolens*.) The Yellow Indian Virgin's Bower, Oriental or Eastern Clematis. A native of Persia, North Asia and the Himalaya of India, introduced into Britain in 1731. D. Vigorous climber of slender shoots to 20 feet, with long pinnate attractive leaves, rather glaucous, and dainty, scented, star-like, soft yellow flowers, of four ovate, downy sepals, and darker stamens, borne freely on slender stalks from the leaf axils in Aug.-Sept., and followed by silky heads of feathered seeds equally attractive. "L. & S. form No. 13342" is a new var. from Tibet, with unique thick waxy, yellow sepalled flowers, nodding and cup-shaped, and borne freely Sept.-Oct.

Prune by cutting back all growth to 4 or 5 feet during winter. Propagate by seeds, cuttings or layers.

OTTO FROEBEL. Hyb. LAN. Raised by M. Lemoine, France, 1865, having very large flowers of greyish-tinted white, with eight broad sepals and brownish stamens, in May-June, and again in Sept.

C. *PANICULATA*. Japanese Virgin's Bower. Introduced from Japan in 1731. D. Very vigorous climber to 30 or 40 feet, with tri- or quin-foliate leaves, of ovate-cordate, entire leaflets, to 4 inches long, and small, four-sepalled, hawthorn-scented, white flowers produced freely in panicles of 4 inches long from the leaf axils in September and October; followed by feathery masses of seed-heads in favourable years. Owing to its late flowering, this species needs the warmest and sunniest of walls and a favourable summer to display its best in Britain, but it succeeds magnificently in Eastern U.S.A. Prune in early spring, cutting shoots back hard to the base of the previous year's growth. Propagate by seeds, cuttings and layers.

C. *PATENS*. (Syn. *C. coerulea*.) A native of Japan, collected by Philipp Franz von Siebold (1796–1844), and introduced to Holland and Britain about 1836. D. Slender climber up to 12 feet, with tri- or quin-foliate leaves consisting of entire, pointed lanceolate leaflets, 2 to 4 inches long, and solitary flowers of six to eight pointed, spreading sepals of white to violet or violet-blue, measuring up to six inches across in May-June. There is a doubt about the species being in cultivation today in its original form, but it is important as a parent of many large-flowered hybrids, especially of "Edouard Desfosse", held to be the largest flowered of them all. The other outstanding hybrids of this class include: "Bagatelle", "Barbara Dibley", "Barbara Jackman", "Baronne de Verdières", "Daniel Deronda", "Etoile de Paris", "Fair Rosamond", "King of the Belgians", "Lady Londesborough", "La Lorraine", "Lasurstern", "Le Cid", "Lord Gifford", "Marcel Moser", "Miss Bateman", "Mrs. George Jackman", "Mrs. P. B. Truax", "M. Koster", "Nelly Moser", "Sir Garnet Wolseley", "The Bride", "The President", "The Queen", and "Xerxes". There is also a larger flowering var. *grandiflora*. Flowers are borne on short growths from the previous year's wood, and pruning may be carried out in the following manner—prune all dead and weak shoots away in late January or February, and shorten the strong shoots retained a little and tie them in; then after flowering, about half the flowered shoots can be pruned back to nodes from which new shoots can develop and be trained to cover the space available. It is best to allow only the strongest shoot at a node to prosper, when two arise.

Propagate by seeds, if seedlings are wanted, but they will be variable and only the best should be retained; by cuttings and layers when true-to-type plants are required.

C. *PAVOLINIANA*. A species from China, introduced by E. H. Wilson (1876–1930) to Britain in 1908. E. Climber up to 15 feet, with tri-foliate leaves, made up of entire, glabrous, ovate leaflets, on long stalks, and small, fragrant, pure white, four-sepalled flowers, about 1½ inches across, in clusters of three to seven from the leaf axils, freely, in June. Over-shadowed by C. *armandii*, and not often seen. May be grown on warm walls or under glass. Prune towards the end of February, thinning out the growth. Propagate by seeds, cuttings and layers.

PERCY PICTON. Hyb. PAT. Very large flowers of rosy-purple from the old wood in June-July; smaller flowers of lighter hue from the young wood in Sept. Named for the raiser, and introduced by J. Fisk, 1956.

PERLE D'AZUR. Hyb. JAC. Large flowers of light sky-blue, somewhat saucer-shaped, and freely produced, June-Aug.

PINK PERFECTION. Variety of C. *montana* v. *rubens* (q.v.).

C. *PITCHERI*. (Syn. C. *cordata*, C. *simsii*.) A native of Colorado and western states of U.S.A., introduced into Britain in 1878. D. Climber of loose straggling habit to 10 feet or more, with downy shoots and leaves of three to seven ovate leaflets, downy beneath, and small, urn-shaped, solitary flowers, about an inch long, purplish-blue on the outside, on downy stalks in May to Sept. The seeds are without the plumose style characteristic of the genus. Prune in February, thinning out the shoots, and reducing those left by about one half their length. Propagate by seeds, cuttings and layers.

POURPRE MAT. Hyb. VIT. l-f. Flowers up to 5 inches across, of a deep, rich violet-purple, in autumn.

PRESIDENT. See THE PRESIDENT.

PRINCE HENDRICK. Hyb. LAN. Large flowers of azure-blue, with pointed sepals, July-Aug.; may be forced under glass.

PRINCESS OF WALES. Hyb. LAN. A rather old form with large flowers of blue and mauve, July-Aug.

PROTEUS. Hyb. FLO. Large flowers of pink, suffused by a soft plum-purple, producing double flowers from the old wood, single from the young, May-July.

C. *QUINQUEFOLIOLATA*. A native of China, 1900. E. Climber to 20 feet, ribbed downy shoots, furnished with quin-foliate leaves, made up of leaflets lanceolate and 2 to 4 inches long, and bearing milk-white, four to six narrow sepalled flowers, about 2 inches across, in cymes of threes, fives or sevens from the leaf axils in Aug.-Sept., followed by decorative seed-heads, with long silky seed-styles. Difficult to obtain. Best on sheltered walls.

C. *RANUNCULOIDES*. Introduced from China, 1906. A herbaceous perennial, with stems growing 4 to 6 feet, tri-foliate or pinnate leaves of coarsely toothed, broad ovate leaflets, and small, four-sepalled flowers of pale rose to purple, with sepals reflexing back, produced singly or in few-flowered panicles from leaf axils and the end of shoots in summer. Prune by cutting to ground level in February. Propagate by seeds and root division.

C. *RECTA*. (Syn. *C. erecta*.) White Herbaceous Virgin's Bower. A native of southern and eastern Europe, introduced in 1597. A herbaceous species with erect stems of 3 to 4 feet high, furnished with glabrous pinnate leaves, made up of five to seven entire, ovate, stalked leaflets of 1 to $2\frac{1}{2}$ inches long, and small, white, fragrant, four-sepalled flowers, freely borne in large, loose terminal and axillary panicles in June-July. Once established, it makes a handsome bush of bloom in the hardy plant border. There are several varieties. Var. *flore pleno* is a good double-flowered form; *grandiflora* displays larger and finer flowers; and *purpurea* has stems and leaves of a bronzy purple. Propagate by seeds, and root division.

C. *REHDERIANA*. (Syn. *C. nutans*, *C. nutans thyrsoides*.) A native of western China, collected by Père George Aubert (c. 1899), but apparently introduced to Britain by E. H. Wilson in 1904. The Nodding Virgin's Bower. D. Vigorous climber up to 25 feet, suitable to grow through trees or tall shrubs, or on arbours, pergolas and porches, with long pinnate leaves, consisting of seven or nine coarsely toothed or lobed, cordate-ovate leaflets, of 2 to 3 inches long, and delightful nodding, bell-like, pale yellow flowers, cowslip-scented, about $\frac{3}{4}$ inch long, in erect, downy panicles, up to 9 inches long, freely produced from the leaf axils in Sept.-Oct. Prune severely in the winter; a good plan being to retain a framework of main shoots and prune all laterals back to the first node from the base. Propagate by seeds, cuttings and layers.

ROYAL VELOURS. Hyb. VIT. l-f. Medium flowers of a rich, deep, velvety reddish-purple, produced very abundantly in July-Sept.

RUBELLA. Hyb. JAC. Large flowers of a deep claret-purple, June-Sept. Bred in 1865.

*C.* x *RUBRO-MARGINATA.* Hyb. *C. flammula* x *C. viticella.* D. Climber to about 12 feet, resembling *C. flammula* in habit, but bearing white flowers, margined with reddish-violet, and with six sepals about 1½ inches across, sweetly scented, and produced abundantly from about August onwards. Prune hard in February, cutting last year's shoots to their base. Propagate by cuttings and layers for increase.

SENSATION. Hyb. LAN. Very large flowers of six or seven sepals of a satiny pale greyish blue to mauve; raised 1867.

*C. SERRATIFOLIA.* Cut-leaf Clematis. A native of Korea, introduced into Britain in 1918, but still rather rare. D. Climber with slender stems to 10 feet, with doubly ternate leaves, made up of sharply toothed, glabrous, ovate leaflets of 1½ to 3 inches length, and solitary flowers produced in twos or threes from the leaf axils, similar to those of *C. tangutica*, with four soft yellow narrow sepals about an inch long, in Aug.-Sept., followed by silky seed heads of equal attraction. Prune severely in Jan.-Feb., cutting back the previous year's growth to the base. Propagate by seeds which germinate fairly quickly, and by cuttings and layers.

*SIEBOLDII.* Var. of *C. florida* (q.v.).

*SIEBOLDII.* Hyb. PAT. Large flowers of lavender-blue, with centre of brown stamens, May-Aug. Apparently a hybrid of continental origin, not often offered in Britain.

*C. SIMSII.* Synonym of *C. pitcheri* (q.v.).

SIR GARNET WOLSELEY. Hyb. PAT. Large flowers of blue and bronzy-purple, with red bars down the middle of the sepals, in May-Aug.

SNOWDRIFT. Var. of *C. armandii* (q.v.).

*C. SONGARICA.* A native of Siberia and Northern Asia, collected in 1880. D. Sub-shrub, with herbaceous stems of 4 to 5 feet, furnished with simple, narrow, linear to lanceolate leaves of 2 to 4 inches long, and a bright bluish-green; bearing small, yellowish white flowers freely in long-stalked clusters from leaf axils and ends of shoots, July-Oct., often succeeded by silky seed heads. Prune by cutting away growth to ground level in winter. Propagate by seeds.

SOLDAT INCONNU. Hyb. FLO. Semi-double flowers of the purest white, June-Sept.

*C. SPOONERI.* (Syn. *C. chrysocoma* v. *sericea*.) An outstanding species introduced from China in 1909. D. Climber, vigorous to 20 feet, with shoots and stalked, tri-foliate leaves of long, ovate, coarsely toothed leaflets, covered when young with a pale yellowish-brown hairy down of pleasing bronzy appearance when young, and four-sepalled white flowers, 3 to 4 inches wide, produced on long stalks, singly or in pairs from the leaf axils in May-June. There is a var. *rosea*, less easy to come by, with delightful apple-blossom pink blooms. Prune during the winter, thinning out and regulating the shoots to furnish the space available. Propagate by seeds, cuttings and layers.

*C. STANDISHII.* This Clematis is now regarded as a variety of *C. patens*, with large lavender-blue flowers in May-July, and has been used in hybridisation.

*C. STANLEYI.* Synonym of *Clematopsis stanleyi*. A South African semi-woody shrub, that differs from the Clematis in having the sepals of the flower overlapping (imbricate), whereas those of Clematis are separate to the base (valvate), and is thus given a separate genus. The plant is capable of growing to 6–8 feet, with hairy shoots and hairy pinnate leaves of pinnate or lobed leaflets, and hanging flowers of four overlapping, ribbed, pink to pale purple sepals, about 2½ inches long, on strong, erect stalks of 7 to 10 inches from the leaf axils, in Aug.-Sept., followed by seed-heads of silky silvery-white. It is a plant for greenhouse culture. Prune by cutting back shoots hard in late winter. Propagate by seeds and cuttings.

*C. STANS.* Introduced from Japan, 1860, by Phillip Franz von Siebold (1796–1866). D. A sub-shrub of non-climbing herbaceous habit, making erect, greyish-downy stems to 2 feet, with opposite, ternate leaves, with large coarsely and sharply toothed leaflets, and small, pale blue, tubular flowers with the ends of the sepals reflexed back, in long-stalked, terminal and axillary clusters in September; very similar to *C. heracleifolia*, but of looser and less distinguished habit. Propagate by seed and division.

STAR OF INDIA. Hyb. JAC. Large reddish-plum coloured flowers, fading to violet-purple, with red bar down the middle of the sepals, July-Aug. 1867.

STELLA. Hyb. PAT. Introduced in 1871. Flowers of light-violet or deep mauve, with reddish-plum bar to each of the eight sepals, and chocolate anthers, primrose-scented, June-Sept.

C. *TANGUTICA.* (Syn. *C. orientalis* v. *tangutica.*) A native of Western Mongolia and North Western China, introduced in 1898. D. Climber with slender stems up to 10 feet, furnished with pinnate leaves of glaucous green, raggedly toothed leaflets, and the most charming nodding, solitary flowers, produced on long stalks, and made up of four-ovate sepals, slender-pointed and a glowing yellow, Aug.-Oct., followed by silvery, shining seed-heads, the earliest intermingled with the latest flowers. A delightful species for roving over boulders or large rocks or through shrubs or trees in the rock garden. Var. *obtusiuscula* has smaller leaflets, and the sepals of its lantern-like flowers are somewhat smaller and blunter, but of deeper yellow. "Grave-tye variety", a selected form of v. *obtusiuscula*, is the best of these handsome yellow-flowering Clematis for today's garden. Prune hard back in February to the base of the previous year's growth. Propagate by seeds, cuttings and layers.

C. *TEXENSIS.* (Syn. *C. coccinea.*) The Scarlet Clematis, Leather-flower. A native of Texas, U.S.A., introduced into Britain about 1876. D. A slender climber of charming and distinctive habit, making stems up to 6 feet or more which die back to ground level each winter. The foliage is of pinnate leaves, consisting of four to eight stalked ovate to roundish glabrous leaflets, bi- or tri-lobed, and the flowers are solitary on 5 to 6 inch slender stalks, nodding and urn or pitcher-shaped, about an inch long, made up of thick, somewhat leathery sepals, reflexed at the tips, varying in colour from red, to scarlet, or carmine, and attractive for some considerable period between July and October. In its native country it is said to grow to 24 feet or more, and to stand up to temperatures of 20 degrees below zero, but in the milder moister climate of Britain it is rather more tender, and is best grown on a sheltered south wall outdoors, or in a cold greenhouse. A larger-flowered variety, var. *major*, described by W. Robinson (*The English Flower Garden*) and W. J. Bean (*Trees and Shrubs Hardy in the British Isles*), seems lost to cultivation. The species has, however, been crossed with

*C. patens* and others, to give rise to several handsome, large, open-flowered hybrids of bright rich colours, such as "Admiration", "Countess of Onslow", "Duchess of Albany", "Duchess of York", "Grace Darling", "Gravetye Beauty", and "Sir Trevor Lawrence".

THE BRIDE. Hyb. PAT. Large flowers of gleaming white, with centre of yellow stamens, June-Oct.

THE PRESIDENT. Hyb. PAT. Large flowers with pointed sepals, deep violet with paler bar down the middle of each sepal, and dark brownish anthers; flowering on the old and the young growth, June-Oct.

THE QUEEN. Hyb. PAT. Large flowers of pale lavender, June-Oct.

*C. TRULLIFERA.* A native of western China, apparently not in cultivation. Described as a vigorous deciduous climber of similar habit to *C. montana*, but bearing somewhat larger, creamy-white, four-sepalled flowers in July-Aug. Prune like *C. montana*. Propagate by seeds, cuttings and layers.

*C. TUBULOSA.* Synonym of *C. heracleifolia* (q.v.).

*C. UNCINATA.* Introduced from China in 1901 but seldom seen. Semi-E. Climber to 12 feet, with pinnate or bi-ternate leaves, consisting of entire, oval to lanceolate leaves, strongly veined and glaucous underneath, and small, fragrant, white, four-sepalled flowers, freely borne in terminal and axillary panicles, making large sprays, in June-July. Prune February, thinning and regulating growth. Propagate by seeds, cuttings and layers.

*C. x VEDRARIENSIS.* Hyb. *C. chrysocoma* x *C. montana* var. *rubens*, raised by Vilmorin et Cie, Verrière le Buisson, France, 1914. D. Climber to 20 feet, with tri-foliate leaves, of downy, ovate, coarsely toothed leaflets, and four- to six-sepalled flowers of a delicate rose-pink borne on slender hairy stalks, 4 to 5 inches long, from the leaf axils of the previous years's growth in May. Prune to thin out the growths in February; or if necessary, shorten after flowering. Propagate by seeds, cuttings and layers.

There is a "Highdown Variety", in which the flowers are deeper pink on the reverse.

*C. VEITCHIANA.* A native of China, introduced in 1904 by Messrs. Veitch & Sons. D. Climber to 15 feet, with doubly pinnate leaves of many small ovate, coarsely toothed leaflets, and small, nodding, bell-like, scented, yellowish-white flowers, borne in panicles from the leaf axils in September-October;

similar to *C. rehderiana*, which is distinguished by its single pinnate leaves with larger leaflets. Prune in winter, rather severely. Propagate by seeds, cuttings and layers.

VELUTINA PURPUREA. Hyb. JAC. Large flowers of a rich blackish-purple, with greenish stamens in the centre, July-Oct. Introduced 1866.

VENOSA VIOLACEA. Hyb. VIT. l-f. The flowers are a rich violet with delicate and marked white veining to the base of the sepals, and have dark brown anthers on white filaments in the centre, July-Sept.

C. *VERTICILLARIS*. (Syn. *Atragene americana*.) The Bell Rue. Native of North America, from Quebec and Manitoba to North Carolina, introduced in 1797. D. Climber of 6 to 10 feet, with stalked tri-foliate leaves of small ovate to cordate leaflets, and solitary, four-sepalled flowers, 2 to 3 inches wide, of purplish to purplish-blue hue, and petal-like staminoides, on 3-inch stalks from the axils of the previous year's growth in May. Rather rare, but useful for limited space. Prune after flowering or in winter to thin out growth. Propagate by seeds, cuttings and layers.

VICTORIA. Hyb. JAC. Large flowers of soft heliotrope or pale mauve-purple, almost transparent, July-Aug.

VILLE DE LIMOGES. Hyb. FLO. Large double flowers of pure white, May-June.

VILLE DE LYON. Hyb. VIT. l-f. Large flowers of bright carmine-red, deepening round the edges of the sepals, July-Sept.

C. *VIORNA*. The Leather-flower. A native of the eastern States of U.S.A., introduced as long ago as 1730, and still uncommon, as it is chiefly of botanical interest. D. Semi-woody Climber with slender stems up to 10 feet, which die back each year, furnished with pinnate leaves of glabrous, tri-foliate or tri-lobed leaflets, and solitary, nodding, urn-shaped flowers, of leathery thick sepals, and dull reddish-purple, on stout short stalks about July. Prune by cutting away dead stems in winter. Propagate by seeds.

C. *VIRGINIANA*. American Virgin's Bower. A common native of U.S.A., and Canada, introduced into England in 1767, but although akin to *C. vitalba*, it is inferior to the latter, and is not much grown. D. Climber to 20 feet, with tri-foliate leaves of stalked, coarsely toothed ovate leaflets, and axillary panicles of small, dull white, four-sepalled flowers, about one inch across, often with the sexes on different plants, in Aug.-Sept. Prune in February, hard. Propagate by seeds, cuttings and layers.

*C. VITALBA.* The Traveller's Joy, Old Man's Beard, etc. The only Clematis native to Britain, but also found in Europe and North Africa, chiefly on chalk or limestone soils. D. Climber to 40 feet and more, with long pinnate leaves of five ovate to lanceolate, coarsely toothed to almost entire leaflets, and small, dull greenish white flowers in terminal and axillary panicles in July to September, followed by grey woolly tufted balls of seed-heads which persist well into the winter. Owing to its rampant growth, the plant is best placed in the woodland or wild garden, clambering through old trees or tall shrubs or in hedges, where it can give quite an attractive display. Prune, if desired, in February, cutting hard back. Propagate by seeds, cuttings and layers.

*C. VITICELLA.* Purple Virgin's Bower, Vine Bower. A native of Southern Europe, introduced into England in 1569. D. Climber of rapid growth of about 10 feet, but more under favourable conditions, with pinnate leaves, of tri-foliate leaflets, and abundantly borne, small nodding, saucer-shaped flowers, about $1\frac{1}{2}$ inches across, fragrant and usually purple-blue, but possibly rosy-purple, purple or lavender, solitary or on branched stalks, July to September. The species is variable, and several varieties have been propagated, such as var. *albiflora*, a pure white; var. *alba luxurians*, larger white; var. *coerulea*, blue-violet; var. *flore pleno*, double rose-purple; var. *kermesiana*, bright vinous red, not growing more than 8 feet; var. *rubra grandiflora*, crimson-claret flowers, often double; and var. *nana*, rose-purple, and only 3 feet tall. The species is often used as a stock for grafting on the large-flowered hybrids, especially on the continent, but the practice is not commendable, as it increases the risk of die-back or wilt disease.

Of greater garden interest for their enhanced floral beauty are the hybrids of which *C. viticella* has been a parent. They include small-flowering forms such as "Abundance", "Etoile Violet", "Little Nell", "Minuet"; and large-flowering forms such as "Ascotiensis", "Blue Bell", "Coquette", "Ernest Markham", "Huldine", "Lady Betty Balfour", "Mme Grange", "Mrs. Spencer Castle", "Mme Jules Correvon", "Modesta", "Pourpre Mat", "Royal Velours", "Venosa", and "Ville de Lyon".

Prune by cutting back each year, about February, the previous year's growth to just above a node about 4 to 6 inches from the base. Or if a framework of branches is desired, prune less severely until the framework has been built up, and then prune to the framework. Propagate by seeds, cuttings and layers.

VYVYAN PENNELL. Hyb. LAN. Large double flowers of deep violet blue, suffused purple and carmine at the centre, May-Sept.; introduced 1958, by Pennell & Sons, Ltd.

W. E. GLADSTONE. Hyb. LAN. Very large flowers of lilac with a lighter bar down the middle of each sepal; black anthers on white filaments, July-Aug.

WILLIAM KENNETT. Hyb. LAN. Large lavender flowers, with darker centre, and crimped or wavy edges to the sepals, June-Aug.

XERXES. Hyb. PAT. Large flowers of violet ground, lined with purple, June, Aug.-Oct.

# APPENDIX A

## SELECTIONS OF CLEMATIS
## FOR GARDEN PURPOSES

### *A Clematis for each Month of the Year*

JANUARY – *C. calycina*
FEBRUARY – *C. cirrhosa*
MARCH – *C. armandii*
APRIL – *C. montana*
MAY – *C. indivisa, C.* x *patens* hybrids*
JUNE – *C. chrysocoma, C.* x *florida* hybrids*
*C.* x *lanuginosa* hybrids*
JULY – *C.* x *jackmanii* hybrids*
AUGUST – *C. viticella* hybrids,* *C. campaniflora*
SEPTEMBER – *C. flammula*
OCTOBER – *C. tangutica* (flowers and seed heads)
NOVEMBER – *C. paniculata**
DECEMBER – *C. vitalba* (seed heads)

*\*Bloom for longer than the month.*

### *Twelve Large-Flowering Hybrids*
### *for Borders and Small Gardens*

Belle of Woking, *mauve*
Comtesse de Bouchaud, *pink*
Crimson King, *rosy-red*
Duchess of Edinburgh, *white*
Edouard Defosse, *violet-mauve*
Jackmanii superba, *violet-blue*

Lady Northcliffe, *lavender*
Lasurstern, *deep purplish-blue*
Lincoln Star, *pink and maroon*
Madame Ed. André, *deep red*
Nelly Moser, *pale pink, carmine*
The President, *deep violet*

# Appendix A

## Twelve More for Larger Gardens

Barbara Dibley, *rich violet*

Barbara Jackman, *petunia*

Beauty of Worcester, *bluish-violet*

Bracebridge Star, *lavender*

Gypsy Queen, *rich dark purple*

Henryi, *creamy-white*

Huldine, *pearly-white*

Mrs. Cholmondeley, *light blue*

Mrs. Hope, *satiny mauve*

Proteus, *pink, soft purple*

Ville de Lyon, *carmine-red*

Wm. Kennett, *deep lavender*

## Twelve Vigorous Free-flowering Kinds for Walls and Fences and Mass Effect on Porches and Arbours

Abundance, *soft purple*

C. *chrysocoma, pinkish-white*

C. *flammula, white*

Kermesina, *bright red*

Minuet, *cream and purple*

M. Koster, *rosy-purple*

Pink Perfection, *deep pink*

C. *montana grandiflora, white*

C. *macropetala, lavender*

C. x *jouiniana, yellow-white*

C. *orientalis, yellow*

C. *viticella, purple*

## Twelve Free-flowering Kinds for Woodlands, to grow through Shrubs and Trees and to cover Stumps

C. *campaniflora, white*

C. *chrysocoma, pinkish-white*

C. *flammula, white*

C. *graciliflora, white*

C. *indivisa, white*

C. *montana*, and vars.

C. *rehderiana, pale yellow*

C. *spooneri, white*

C. *tangutica* and vars., *yellow*

C. x *vedrariensis, rose*

C. *vitalba, white*

C. *viticella* and vars.

## Fine Herbaceous Clematis for Borders

C. x *aromatica, bluish-violet*

C. *crispa, bluish-purple*

C. x *durandii, blue-violet*

C. x *eriostemon, deep blue*

C. *heracleifolia, bright blue*

C. *recta* var. *flore pleno, white*

C. *integrifolia, blue*

C. *viticella* var. *nana* (dwarf)

## Appendix A

### Clematis producing Very Large Flowers

Edouard Desfosse, *violet-mauve*
Lasurstern, *purplish-blue*
Madame van Houtte, *white*

Marie Boisselot, *white*
Prince Hendrick, *azure blue*
W. E. Gladstone, *lavender*

### Clematis for the Rock Garden

*C. tangutica* Gravetye variety, over large boulders
*C. viticella* var. *nana*, growing only 3 feet high.
*C. koreana*, decumbent habit over rocks.
*C. alpina*, trained over or up rock faces.
*C. afoliata*, for a sheltered sunny corner in bold rocks.

### Large-flowering Hybrids by Colour

*Blue* – Ascotiensis; Blue Belle; Blue Gem; Countess of Lovelace; Daniel Deronda; Etoile Violette*; Elsa Spath; Lady Londesborough*; Mrs. Cholmondeley; Mrs. P. B. Truax; Perle d'Azur; Prince Hendrick.

*Cream and Purple* – Minuet.

*Lavender* – Lady Northcliffe; W. E. Gladstone; William Kennett.

*Mauve* – Beauty of Richmond; Belle of Woking; Edouard Desfosse; Lady Caroline Nevill*; Lady Londesborough*; Little Nell; Marcel Moser*; Mrs. Hope*; Nelly Moser*; Proteus*; Victoria; Mrs. Spencer Castle; Lincoln Star*.

*Petunia* – Barbara Jackman*; Ernest Markham.

*Purple* – Abundance; Countess of Onslow; Empress of India*; Gipsy Queen; Jackmanii; jackmanii superba; Lady Betty Balfour; Lasurstern; Lord Neville*; Pourpre Mat; Royal Velours.

*Pink* – Comtesse de Bouchard; Fairy Queen*; King George V*; Miss Crawshay; Markham's Pink; M. Koster; Sealand Gem.

*Red* – Crimson King; Grace Darling; Gravetye Beauty; jackmanii rubra; kermesina; Madame Edouard André; Star of India; Ville de Lyon; Duchess of Sutherland.

## Appendix A

*Violet* – Barbara Dibley; Beauty of Worcester; Etoile de Paris; King Edward VII; La France; The President; Xerxes.

*White* – alba luxurians; alpina sibirica; Duchess of Edinburgh; Fair Rosamund; florida bicolor; henryi; Huldine; Lucie Lemoine; Marie Boisselot; Miss Bateman; Mrs. George Jackman\*; Snowdrift; The Bride.

*\* With bars of lighter or deeper colour down the middle of the sepals.*

### Clematis Hybrids which produce Double Flowers

Beauty of Worcester; Countess of Lovelace; Duchess of Edinburgh; Daniel Deronda; Lucie Lemoine; Miriam Markham; Markham's Pink; Proteus; Enchantress; Undine; Vyvyan Pennell.

### Clematis for Scent

*C. afoliata; C. armandii; C. x aromatica; C. chinensis; C. connata; C. crispa; C. flammula; C. ligusticifolia; C. marata; C. orientalis; C. paniculata; C. pavoliniana; C. rehderiana; C. uncinata; C. veitchiana; C. vitalba; C. viticella.*

# APPENDIX B

*George Jackman & Son (Woking Nurseries) Ltd.,*
*Woking,*
*Surrey.*

*Fisk's Clematis Nursery,*
*Westleton,*
*Nr. Saxmundham,*
*Suffolk.*

*Pennell & Sons, Ltd.,*
*Lincoln,*
*Lincolnshire.*

*Hillier & Sons, Ltd.,*
*Winchester,*
*Hampshire.*

# INDEX

# Index

# Index

174

# Index